In Search of the
Unknown Father

A German - Serbian Destiny

Dedicated to

My mother

Frida

And my fathers

Vitomir and Rudolf

\

Wolfgang Petzold

In Search of the
Unknown Father

A war child explores the incredible story of his origins

- A German-Serbian destiny -
- The truth always comes to light

Bibliographic information of the Deutsche Nationalbibliothek:

The German National Library lists this publication in the Deutsche Nationalbibliografie; Detailed bibliographic data are available on the Internet at http://dnb.dnb.de.

© 2018 Wolfgang Petzold

Production and publishing:
BoD - Books on Demand, Norderstedt

ISBN: 978-3-7481-8035-7

Translated from the original German by Cassandra Reeh Taylor
Seattle, WA

Table of Contents

Chapter 1 - Prologue

As I look back at 71 years of my fulfilled and extraordinarily restless life: my childhood, my "Sturm und Drang" years, the before and after conversion, or my many foreign missions with the Bundeswehr, all were nothing, compared to this once elusive story that began in the summer of 2011 and continues to this day.

In my book "Year 44" (published in July 2014 for my 70th birthday) I shared my life, with all my strengths and weaknesses, to readers. Despite a lack of advertising by publishers and sponsors, it found a relatively wide readership. However, I view the following story as the highlight of my life. It rounds out my previous existence and gives me a completely new viewpoint of my past.

I hope to convey the feeling that a piece of German history from 74 years ago, is brought front and center, and is more relevant today than ever before. I want to give people, with similar destinies, the courage and the strength to search for their true roots even after many years have gone by: *Because every human being has the right to know his origin.*

In addition, I would like to raise the neglected theme of "children of prisoners of war" to the public interest. Whenever I was on television, in the newspapers and in lectures, I was told that, while I have had a remarkably extraordinary outcome, public art work as a feature or documentary film cannot be considered because of cost. However, the MDR has a remarkable documentary about an event, "Kühnhaide bei Zwönitz," which unfortunately was only a short video. This book is a renewed attempt to reach a broad readership with my concern.

I have deliberately used many photos and documents to provide authoritative evidence for my story. The many names and dates are not intended to aggravate, but to impart important life data to my children and their descendants. Presenting the last four years chronologically, is the best way to understand what has happened since 1941. The flashbacks to personal and historical backgrounds allow me to clarify relationships which are based on meticulous research that I have conducted over the last four years.

I would like to thank the many people, institutions and public media in Germany, Serbia and Switzerland, who helped me find my father. First and foremost, however, my wife Ilse deserves my utmost gratitude because she repeatedly encouraged me to continue my research in seemingly hopeless situations. Regardless of nationality, everyone, who has lovingly found each other after a long time, has my deepest affection and respect.

I am sharing my story with the hope that it will be memorable for you.

Dresden, October 2015

Chapter 2 - Historical Flashback

Reflecting about the year 1941, specifically April 6th, Hitler's Air Force bombarded the capital of Serbia, Belgrade. Tens of thousands of people lost their lives. Within a few days, Serbia surrendered on April 18th to the overpowering German military machine. About 250,000 Serbian soldiers were captured, with about 150,000 deported to Germany. These prisoners were used for forced labor, especially with farmers in the countryside.

Twenty-eight of these men arrived in the small village of Kühnhaide, Zwönitz Kreis Aue. I was born in that village on the 23rd of July 1944. While researching the lives of 20 of the prisoners, I came across historical events that still make me distrust people today. Here are just a few examples: At the beginning of the Yugoslavia /Serbian campaign, 2,370 innocent people were killed in the towns of Kraljevo and 1,700 in Kragujevac. An entire grammar school with over 300 students and teachers were executed. I became aware of such atrocities from Pancevo, Smederevka, Palanka to Selevac. In total, 80,000 people were killed in the Serbian territory or taken as hostages by the Wehrmacht, many of whom were Jews. Almost 2 million people in Serbia which was part of Yugoslavia (about 10% of the population at that time) lost their lives during the Second World War.

In contrast, Serbian soldiers taken as German prisoners had a comparatively "better" chance of survival. As I have discovered in recent years, many of them had the choice: to be burned by the German Wehrmacht during the bloody battles or to go into captivity. Most of them took the supposedly better route of captivity.

In Kühnhaide, the Serbs were treated as prisoners and exposed to all sorts of inhumane treatment, but they had a good chance of returning home. The Serbian soldiers usually replaced the German landowners, who had been killed at the front or on the farm. According to statements from surviving eyewitnesses, they worked diligently and set the daily routines on the farms. During this time, it was not difficult to understand that interpersonal relationships started. Such liaisons were, of course, prohibited and would incur strict punishment. Those secrets continue to be kept today and proved to be a stumbling block for my research. Even after more than 70 years, these interactions are still considered taboo and not discussed. Nevertheless, I was fortunate enough to have won the trust of many residents who were willing to exchange information with me.

Until July 19, 1941, most Serbian prisoners of war were captured in Sarajevo as were father Svetozar (born 1897) and son Radojica Miljkovic (born 1919). Only after the war did they learn that they had been imprisoned at the same time for four years in German camps. The father in the Deputies VI D (Dortmund), Nuremberg- Langwasser and the Officers' Camp XIII B (Hammelburg) and the son in Stalag VIII A (Oberlausitz, Görlitz) and most recently Stalag IV B (Mühlberg, near Dresden).

I learned from Radojica's daughters Branislava and Natalija that their father, Radojica, narrowly escaped execution in 1941. He was on a short visit to his parents in Smederevka, Palanka, and saw how innocent people were rounded up indiscriminately. I have seen footage by German defense photographer Gerhard Gronefeld, documenting such incredible criminal cruelty in Pancevo. He was perplexed about the behavior that his film documented.

As a memorial and as a reminder, I have written about these Serbian prisoners and placed my search in the center of their story. I investigated the following Serbian prisoners of war very meticulously. The reader will encounter their names more often in the course of my remarks. I thank you, my dear Serbian "countrymen," who have preserved so much humanity, courage, modesty and love in such a horrific time:

> Sergeant Precanica,
> Milan Sergeant Jovanovic,
> Zivko Sergeant Colic,
> Velizar Sergeant Simic,
> Slavoljub Sergeant Boskovic,
> Vitomir Soldier Vrancevic,
> Vojislav Soldier Jovanovic,
> Vlastimir Soldier Miljkovic,
> Radojica (called "Zeppelin")

A poem by Zeppelin, written around 1943, bears witness to the yearning of young people for their homeland and their loved ones.

A truly historical document:

MEMORY

Like a flower falls in the cold winter
This is how our youth goes
And is drowned with great pain.

Group photo of all 28 Serbs in Kühnhaide - Winter 41/42

On the back of this photo Radojica Miljkovic wrote his poem.

Farewell to the Serbs on May 9, 1945

Haymaking: 3 peasants and a Serb

The accommodations of the Serbian prisoners of war,
are almost unchanged in 2011

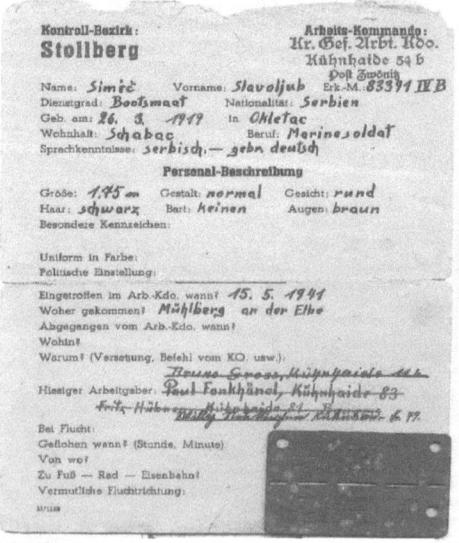

Recognition card of a prisoner

Replacement money for prisoners

<u>Chapter 3 – Prehistory</u>

Golden wedding anniversary photo of Wolfgang's grandparents,
Wolfgang is at the far left.

19 years old   70 years old

When looking at these photos, I cannot help but wonder about the 19 year old's ancestry. Ever since we got together, my wife Ilse always wanted to know about my heritage because I did not look like the rest of the "Kellers" and "Petzolds". For decades, I successfully avoided this whole discussion. I saw no reason at all to doubt my origin. If anyone even hinted at the topic at some point, my parents always claimed that I looked like grandmother Martha from Neudorf or grandfather Reinhard from Kühnhaide. After all these of years, it is difficult to see the similarity today, but I remember in my youth, I was often considered a Frenchman or an Italian.

In family gatherings in the fifties, even my dear Aunt Else, now at the tender age of 91, used to refer to me as the "charming Frenchman" in front of everyone. Did she know something about my origin? Why did she say that in my parent's presence? In any case, it was clear to Ilse that my roots had to lie in the Mediterranean range. She even guessed that I might have been adopted in the war, was the victim of postwar mishaps or that one of my ancestors came from another country. When our sons, Robert and Sascha were born, doctors and nurses were amazed by their exceptionally dark complexions, black hair and eyebrows.

An event in the mid-90s has been particularly memorable for me.
Living in Berlin with his family, our son Sascha came up with special idea for his birthday: He invited Ilse and me to a beautiful Turkish restaurant. It was an unforgettable experience. I have always been quite friendly and willing to communicate with other people. We immediately got into a conversation with an exceedingly obliging Turkish waiter. He served us quickly and was very attentive. I was a bit startled when he said, very loudly and seriously, "Tell me, sir, when are you going to fly back to Anatolia to be with your relatives? " We found the situation very funny, and Ilse felt that her guesses were validated. Even though we had paid the check, we lingered at least another two hours visiting together in the restaurant.

From that time forward, I often wondered what part of this notion could be true. Due to the constraints of time and my profession, I pushed these thoughts out of my mind. It was not until approximately 2005 that these considerations surfaced again. Ilse, dove deeper into her and our history with her genealogy and the creation of her family tree.

She discovered in mid-2011, that she was the direct descendant (12 generations away) of the legendary master Adam Ries considered the "father of modern arithmetic." When the documents arrived from Adam Ries, Annaberg Federal, I had no doubts either.

My dear Ilse began to pressure me to research and complete the open branches of my family tree. Her confirmation of ancestry to Adam Ries created the impetus for me to learn more about my life than I had examined before. From then on, I began to deal more intensely with this problem and the search for my roots began.

Initially, of course, I researched on the Internet. I learned that August the Strong had a Turkish regiment stationed in Saxony around 1700. After that, I realized that my grandmother Martha from Neudorf had to come from this same line, and that, as a result, I had to be regarded as Turkish-born. Looking closer at the old photos of my grandmother's family, we definitely ruled out that theory because they had no Mediterranean features. So, we determined to search in another direction.

A dog friend, whom we often met at the "dog walk", is very well read and knew my request. One day he showed me a newspaper clipping of the "SZ" with an article about Saxon mining at the time of August the Strong. We

Source: Wikipedia

read that in the 18th century, the importance of mining increased rapidly and miners from a small Italian tribe, called the "whales," came to Saxony. Because the tunnels were drilled manually, shorter people were more suitable for the task. Consequently, excellent diminutive workers were recruited from Italy.

From then on, the "whales" became the favorites in the search for my roots,

because I am only a medium-sized person. I laughed heartily when I saw drawings and pictures of these people. With pointed hats as headgear, these little Italians crept to their ore deposits.

But the whole story took a different turn. Chance was the godfather, and an incredible story began, bordering on a miracle.

Chapter 4 - Miracles Exist - The Chronology of an Odyssey

In a beautiful weekend, on the 16th of July 2011, my unusual journey into my past began. Ilse had managed to prod me out of my lethargy and send me on a trip to my birthplace Kühnhaide, to find family tree documents. Weeks before, I had spent a day investigating my past in Neudorf / Kreis Annaberg. Researching old documents from the Petzold and König relatives brought some family connections to light, but my most urgent question could not be answered.

In Kühnhaide my beaming Aunt Else, whom I had not seen for a long time, produced a large box of photos and documents and was ready to answer all my questions. Much to my astonishment, she knew all the information about my siblings and close relatives by heart. I was able to connect many of my previously hidden family ties. After exploring all familial events for about two hours, my briefcase was full of documents, photos, and notes; but my head was full of emotions. I learned some new information about my childhood and my aunt reminded of other events I had forgotten. Finally, I brought up the question: "Where is my birth house?"

That question was the beginning of my incredible search for my roots. My parents' house was about 300 meters away from my aunt's house, in the direction of Oberdorf, at Lößnitzer Straße 55. There, my parents had rented an apartment on the second floor of the Selig family. We lived there until about 1947, when we moved to another home in Kühnhaide. Shortly thereafter, my father Rudolf got a new job at the Zwönitzer sawmill on the Ellerlein street, so we moved again. Until then, I believed that my parents had a harmonious marriage and that my 14-year-old sister, whom I seldom saw, began teaching as a kindergarten teacher.

Birthplace in Kühnhaide

After visiting my aunt, I drove my Peugeot 207 a few meters to the site of my birth, parked at the side of the road, crossed the street and took some photos of this historic place. Coincidentally, a woman about my age must have watched me investigate the house. She approached me and I informed her why I was photographing the residence. She responded with a few minutes of absolute silence (that's how it seemed to me at least) and then she reacted with a flood of recognition. She hugged me and introduced herself. Her name was Gisela and she had been living in this house at the same time as my family. Two years older than me, she knew me from childhood. She was the one who often pushed me in a handcart through the village. In retrospect, this unexpected contact was the overture to my incredible journey into the past.

Playmates with handcart

Gisela knew a lot about my father Rudolf, my mother Frida, sister Inge and me. Initially, she related some superficial information: I was a cute, bit chubby child, who outwardly did not resemble my sister. Before my birth, my parents seemed compatible and communicated well with each other, were close friends with the landlords, the family Selig. Days later, however, the tide seems to have turned. Almost every day they were quarreling and had many conflicts. My "old and now new girlfriend" told me a lot of details that her mother had told her shortly before death. After that information, I concluded why there was a sudden change of mood in the Petzold family.

My mother Frida was a young and attractive woman. In 1941, at the age of 33, Rudolf was released from military service due to a hip complaint. One could imagine that both of them lived happily ever after, in this difficult time of war. That assumption could have been applied to the time before July 23, 1944, my date of birth. After that, interpersonal rifts probably arose between them, about which I can only speculate, based on my investigations.

During wartime it was quite common for the women of the village to work with the many farmers in the village (approximately 20 farms existed in Kühnhaide at that time) or at the very least, the women would help out at harvest time. Such a scenario was very possible for my mother with the Hennig farm, because the farm was only about 50 meters away from the my parent's apartment. The work was remunerated in kind (eggs, bread, wheat, sausage, meat) to the helpers.

Gisela now proceeded to the core of her history lesson. It sounded something like this: "I do not know if it's right, what I'm telling you now. My mother told me that your mother, Frida, worked for the farmer, Hennig, and was "totally crazy" about Zeppelin who also worked for the Hennig. Then Gisela told me that in Kühnhaide quite a few prisoners of war were working for farmers, and that Zeppelin and another captive worked in the field and property. They had replaced the caretakers who had mostly been at the front or were killed on the farm. Hesitantly, she added, "If you have time, I can show you something." Awareness began to creep into my heart, which would determine my further life. Not three minutes later, Gisela appeared with a large box under her arm, set it down on a garden bench and asked me to sit own. My sitting down was necessary, because based on what followed; I would not have been able to stand up.

My mother Frida and sister Inge arriving from the Hennig farm

Chapter 4.1. - Zeppelin

When Gisela brought out the large box, it contained documents, newspapers and photos. Sitting at the top, was a 1995 newspaper clipping and photograph, and I froze. I looked at the face of Zeppelin and recognized what appeared to be my likeness:

The "Zwönitzer Wochenblatt" published the following article with the photo of Zeppelin with the heading "50 Years since the End of the Second World War"

"Our historical photo comes from the time of the end of the war, recorded around 1944/45. It shows one of the Serbian prisoners of war who, like French and soldiers of other nations, were employed in agriculture. Because of his name, which was difficult to pronounce for the German tongue, he got the nickname "Zeppelin", which probably sounded similar.

The Serbs were housed in Kühnhaide and guarded by Landsturmmann* who were not rigid, so the prisoners had quite a few freedoms.

They worked in Kühnhaide and also in Lenkersdorf with the farmers, who were happy to have manpower, since their own sons were at war.

Little is known about the subject of prisoners of war in Zwönitz, but apart from the inflexible Nazis who harassed them and whose own citizens also had to watch out for themselves, the Zwönitz were generally respectable to them."

(Zwönitzer Wochenblatt 15/1995 of April 1995)

* The Austro-Hungarian *Landsturm* was
a reserve force that consisted of men aged 34
to 55. It was intended to provide replacements
for the front line units and provide a militia for
local defense.
(https://en.wikipedia.org/wiki/Landsturm)

"Zeppelin"

My emotions were a total mess and I
was unaware of the immediate implications. Could it be that there was a connection between me and this Serbian soldier who looked like me? This soldier had worked for the farmer Hennig, and my mother had worked for the

same farmer. My parents had never told me about Serbian prisoners of war in Kühnhaide. All this information was beyond me.

We rummaged through this box for a while. Even though the dreadful thoughts were not entirely new, I realized I had found something unique here. Before I said goodbye to Gisela, she offered to help me in any way to clarify my past. We hugged each other warmly and with a "good luck" I left to ask my Aunt Else once again about my new findings and this newspaper now in my possession. Else was a young woman then, and the siblings had certainly confided with each other.

Arriving at her door, I held the newspaper "under her nose." She had only one comment: "But that was it!" I interpreted her comment to mean it must have been another. At the same time, she corrected herself, claiming that she had never seen a Serb in Kühnhaide, and besides, my mother would not have done such a thing anyway. That was their story, but my suspicions began to grow. What remained was the urge for truth.

With a completely unknown but pleasant feeling, I set off on the way back to Dresden via Oberwiesenthal, planning to do some research there. At the foot of the Pöhlberg at Annaberg, I gave in to a human urge and got out in the first best parking lot. Again, one of those unfortunate coincidences came to me that day: It was my former class teacher, the dear, old Gottfried Rothe, with his wife. I had to tell him immediately about all my new experiences. I felt as if my heart was in my throat.

Almost the same minute I called my wife in Dresden and said confusedly: "I have him!" By that I meant my father. It was still going to be a long way, filling several files and taking many months to final clarity. But how to proceed now? Could a DNA test with my still living sister (who has since unfortunately died) bring certainty?

I got in touch with the renowned laboratory "Galantos Genetics" in Mainz and did a saliva test with my sister Inge. The result came in early December and prompted further steps. It definitely turned out that Inge is just my half-sister.

Here is an excerpt from the DNA test:

Report for Mr. Wolfgang Petzold

Summary:
A posteriori probabilities (W values) of this analysis were calculated on the basis of equal a priori probabilities for the established hypotheses.
Systems W1 W2 W3 PCR Systems 2.593041% 75.398966% 22.007993%
Total 2.593041% 75.398966% 22.007993%
The calculation of the established hypotheses shows, with a probability of 75.4%, that the two persons tested are half-siblings. The probability that the two persons examined are full siblings is 2.59%.
There is a 22% probability that the persons examined are not related to each other.
We assure that the kinship assessment and the kinship probability calculations were performed according to the current scientific evidence.

Mainz, 06th December 2011

For all of us there was only one explanation: "Zeppelin" had to be my father. But what was his real name, was he still alive? There were many questions to answer. Gisela immediately took the lead and gathered people who knew their way around the city or who were alive at that time.

Hellmut Kunz and Anneliese (the girlfriend and neighbor of Gisela's, a Serbian child) were such. None, not even the descendants of the farmer Hennig, knew the name of "Zeppelin" and knew what had become of him.
We were about to give up until we came into contact with the journalist Ms. Muth from the local editorial department of the "Freie Presse" Stollberg. She miraculously offered me support in my search using her journalistic methods. We met in Zwönitz in the Cafe Am Markt, where she began her first interview for about two hours. Everything that I have learned so far, I told her. We dealt intensively with my topic.

After a few days, the first article about my search appeared. I had a good feeling that we would succeed. Later, Ms. Muth accompanied me to all my stations in search of my father. Several articles appeared about it. Here is just one of many:

„Stollberger Zeitung" 17.11.2011

Auf der Suche nach dem richtigen Namen

Ein gebürtiger Kühnhaider glaubt, auf einem alten Foto seinen leiblichen Vater erkannt zu haben. Nun will er mehr erfahren.

VON FRANZISKA MUTH

KÜHNHAIDE – Wolfgang Petzold sucht einen Namen. Wie heißt der Mann auf dem Foto? Der gebürtige Erzgebirger weiß es nicht. Aber er ist sich sicher, und zwar „hundertprozentig": Das Bild zeigt nicht nur einen serbischen Kriegsgefangenen, der in den 1940er-Jahren in Kühnhaide arbeiten musste – es zeigt auch Petzolds leiblichen Vater.

Die Geschichte beginnt im Juli dieses Jahres. Wolfgang Petzolds Frau Ilse – das Paar wohnt heute in Dresden – beschäftigt sich mit Ahnenforschung, ist mit ihrem Stammbaum im 12. Jahrhundert angekommen. Auch Wolfgang Petzold, geboren im Zwönitzer Ortsteil Kühnhaide, will mehr über seine Wurzeln erfahren und recherchiert. Doch schon bei seinem Vater Rudolf Petzold (1905-1981) ist Schluss, ein Stammbuch nicht aufzutreiben. „Wir haben gedacht, das kann doch nicht weg sein", sagt der 67-Jährige. Wolfgang Petzold telefoniert mit Bekannten in Zwönitz – ohne Erfolg. Er beschließt, sein Geburtshaus in Kühnhaide aufzusuchen.

„Habe mich wiedererkannt"

Vor Ort, am 26. Juli, kommt er beim Fotografieren mit den heutigen Bewohnern ins Gespräch – und man drückt ihm ein Zwönitzer Wochenblatt in die Hand, mit dem Hinweis: „Ich zeig dir mal was." Es ist die Ausgabe 15 aus dem Jahr 1995. Auf Seite 14 ein Foto – das Foto. „Sofort war mir dieser junge Mann in Uniform sympathisch", sagt Petzold. Er schaut genauer hin. „Da hat es mich fast weggedroschen, ich musste mich erstmal setzen. Ich habe mich in seinen Augen wiedererkannt."

Laut Wochenblattbericht wurde das Foto gegen Ende des Zweiten Weltkrieges aufgenommen, 1944 oder 1945. Es zeigt einen serbischen Kriegsgefangenen, der in der Landwirtschaft eingesetzt war. Man nannte ihn „Zeppelin" – wohl wegen des für Deutsche schwierig auszusprechenden serbischen Namens. Wolfgang Petzold spricht mit noch mehr Leuten vor Ort. Er findet heraus, dass Zeppelin beim benachbarten Bauern Bruno Hennig gearbeitet hat. Wahrscheinlich war er mit anderen serbischen Gefangenen in einem ehemaligen Stall im Ort untergebracht, wohl von 1942 bis 1945.

„Aus den Aussagen noch lebender und kürzlich verstorbener Personen weiß ich: Mit diesem Mann hatte meine Mutter ein Verhältnis", erzählt Wolfgang Petzold. Dass Frida Petzold (1908-1990) von dem Serben bedrängt wurde, schließt ihr Sohn aus. Er nennt weitere Fakten, die ihn in der Überzeugung bestärken, dass Zeppelin sein leiblicher Vater ist. Geboren wurde Wolfgang Petzold am 23. Juli 1944 in Kühnhaide. Damals sei es üblich gewesen, dass ein Sohn als zweiten Vornamen den ersten Vornamen seines Vaters erhielt. „Ich hätte also eigentlich Rudolf heißen müssen, heiße aber Egon." Er fragt sich, warum sich seine Eltern in den schweren Kriegsjahren noch ein zweites Kind „angeschafft haben, zumal meine Schwester Inge da schon 14 Jahre alt war". Petzold erinnert sich auch an ein Urteil seiner Frau. Als diese zum ersten Mal ihre Schwiegereltern traf, da habe sie – wegen fehlender Ähnlichkeit – gesagt: „Das kann nicht sein." Und schließlich habe er als junger Mann so ausgesehen wie der Zeppelin auf dem Foto, und auch seine beiden Söhne seien das „blanke Ebenbild".

Wolfgang Petzold recherchiert jetzt in alle Richtungen. Vielleicht existiert irgendwo noch eine Arbeitskarte, auf der der richtige Name von Zeppelin vermerkt ist. Er glaubt, dass sich der Name von einem serbischen Vornamen ableitet, vielleicht von Zivadin. Im Kreisarchiv in Aue ist er nicht fündig geworden, auch in der Stadtverwaltung Zwönitz und im Sächsischen Staatsarchiv in Dresden finden sich keine Dokumente. Teilweise sind seine Anfragen noch in Arbeit, so etwa bei der Serbischen Botschaft in Berlin und beim Internationalen Suchdienst im hessischen Bad Arolsen. Auch an die Deutsche Dienststelle für die Benachrichtigung der nächsten Angehörigen von Gefallenen der ehemaligen deutschen Wehrmacht hat er sich gewandt. In einem Schreiben wird ihm von einem serbischen Mitgefangenen in Kühnhaide namens Živko Jovanovic berichtet. Vielleicht war dieser ein Freund von Zeppelin? Jovanovic stammte aus der serbischen Stadt Kruševac. Ein Schreiben an die ehemalige Adresse dieses Mannes kam zurück mit dem Vermerk „Empfänger unbekannt". Ein Brief an den Bürgermeister blieb bisher unbeantwortet.

Nun hat ein serbischer Journalist Petzold versprochen, bei der Suche zu helfen. Er wohnt in Deutschland, sein Großvater wurde von 1941 bis 1944 im Kriegsgefangenenlager Nürnberg-Langwasser festgehalten.

Das Foto ist verschwunden

Das Foto, das 1995 im Wochenblatt erschien und auf dem vielleicht ein entscheidender Hinweis vermerkt sein könnte, ist nicht aufzutreiben. Harald Schindler, Leiter der Gebhardischen Sammlung in der Austel-Villa, hat den Beitrag verfasst. „Ich habe mir das Foto sicher damals geborgt und dann zurückgegeben", sagt er. Aber an wen – das weiß er nicht mehr. Und in seiner Archivkiste sei es ebenfalls nicht.

„Sie haben diese Last ihr ganzes Leben mit sich herumgetragen und ihr Geheimnis mit ins Grab genommen", sagt Wolfgang Petzold über seine Eltern Rudolf und Frida. Wäre der „Fehltritt" seiner Mutter bekannt geworden, so hätte das sicher schlimme Folgen gehabt: „Meine Mutter wäre ins Gefängnis oder ins KZ gekommen, ich ins Heim. Und den serbischen Gefangenen hätte man an die Wand gestellt." Fragt man heute Kühnhaider, so bestätigen diese: „Über so etwas wurde damals nicht gesprochen."

Wolfgang Petzold gibt nicht auf. „Das ist so ein Zufall im Leben, den gibt es nur einmal." Den Mann schätzt er auf dem Foto auf etwas über 20 Jahre. Theoretisch könnte er noch leben, vielleicht ist er knapp über 90. Aber wie ging sein Weg nach der Gefangenschaft weiter, ist er in seine Heimat zurückgekehrt und wenn ja, wo liegt diese?

„Ich würde auf jeden Fall zu ihm fahren, auch an sein Grab", sagt Wolfgang Petzold. Doch bei allem, was der Dresdener noch herausfindet und was ihm verborgen bleibt – eines betont er, wenn er über die zwei Menschen spricht, die ihn großgezogen haben: „Ich bin ihnen nicht böse. Meine Eltern waren die besten Eltern der Welt."

WER BEI DER SUCHE behilflich sein möchte, kann sich melden unter Telefon: 0351 8025637 oder E-Mail: w.petzold@gmx.net.

Wolfgang Petzold vor seinem Geburtshaus im Zwönitzer Ortsteil Kühnhaide. FOTO: ANDREAS WENDT

Das Foto des serbischen Kriegsgefangenen. Petzold ist sich sicher: Dieser Mann ist sein Vater. FOTO: PRIVAT

Balkanfeldzug bedeutete für viele Serben die Gefangenschaft

Im April 1941 griff die Wehrmacht das Gebiet des damaligen Jugoslawien, also auch Serbien, an. Bereits bei den Luftangriffen auf Belgrad starben dabei mehrere tausend Menschen. Nach der baldigen Kapitulation wurde Serbien unter deutsche Militärverwaltung gestellt, während Zehntausende von serbischen Soldaten als Kriegsgefangene genommen wurden – viele davon wurden als Zwangsarbeiter nach Deutschland verschleppt und mussten etwa in der Rüstungsindustrie oder Landwirtschaft arbeiten. Tägliche Arbeitszeiten von zwölf Stunden und lagerartige Unterbringung waren für die meisten normal. Trotz strenger Bewachung kam es natürlich vor, dass Zwangsarbeiter Verhältnisse mit deutschen Frauen eingingen. Dies war allerdings für beide Seiten mit großen Risiken verbunden: Der sogenannte „Verbotene Umgang" konnte für den Zwangsarbeiter die Todesstrafe, für die Frau Diffamierung und Zuchthaus bedeuten.

Newspaper article from Stollberger Zeitung, November

One day, however, a breakthrough came unexpectedly: a Mr. Helmut Simon (83) from Kühnhaide came to me. He had fled from East Prussia in early 1945 and continued his apprenticeship as a 17-year-old with Tailor Arnold in Zwönitz am Markt. He immediately recognized "Zeppelin" as his instructor (He was a tailor by profession) and knew his name: Radojica Miljkovic. What a surprise! How important the role of the press and the viewing public is! Immediately I requested a search order at the German office in Berlin.

Mr. Simon described Radojica as a loving, intelligent, and industrious person who mastered his tailoring skills perfectly.

Helmut Simon in the "Free Press" Stollberg

My new friends Anneliese and Gisela

My dear new friend Hellmut Kunz

In response to my request, the Berlin office informed me that Radovica was admitted to the Prisoners of War Reserve Laboratory in Hohenstein-Ernstthal in November 1943. Other documents could not be found. However, birthplace, date and parents were identified. Some time later, I was told that his father Svetozar was also imprisoned in Germany, in Nuremberg-Langwasser. Both did not learn about their simultaneous imprisonment until after the war.

Further research was carried out via the International Search Service Bad Arolsen, the Serbian Embassy in Berlin, the District Office in Aue, and the Saxon State Archives in Dresden u.v.a.m. By chance I read on the internet that the Serbian journalist Milorad Zivojnov (working in Bonn) was researching this problem. His uncle was also interned. Immediately I contacted Milorad and he became my comrade in this beginning research phase.

About half a year went by until I had one of my "crazy" ideas again (in the end I realized that discovering my destiny was a chain of coincidences and miracles.). On the Internet, I looked up the directory of Belgrade, searched the name "Miljkovic" and found over 1000 entries. The name "Radojica Miljkovic" appeared only once. Was that a hint of fate? As a precaution, I put down a few phrases in Croatian, English and Russian on a piece of paper, as well as the area code of Serbia and some cheap codes. My heart was racing, because I was very excited.

Would that be the starting point for the solution of my problem? The one "up there" was certainly involved as well. When at the other end of the line a friendly, youthful and male voice answered. My short questions in English were:

"Do you know Radojica Miljkovic?"   - Answer: "Yes!"

"Where is he now?"   - Answer: "Not here!"

"When will he come back?"   - Answer: "No more, he is in the coarse (cemetery) "

To my great surprise, the grandson Aleksa (age 17) came forward. I let him know that I was calling from Germany and looking for this Radojica. I could not tell him why I was asking, just that in a few minutes a man called Zivojnov would explain everything because he was a Serb and spoke the language.

Milorad Zivojnov then arranged everything else and made contact. The next day (January 25, 2012) the first e-mails were exchanged. Initially, they were translated by Milorad, then with "Google translation." Branislava (age 51) and Natalija (age 56) later told me that they were ecstatic when they learned of my intentions. The former is a professor at a Belgrade institute and the second a high school teacher; by the way, very attractive women.

We exchanged all the existing documents and photos so that everyone could get an idea, as to why I suspected that Radojica was my father. After both women (and their families) calmed down a bit, we decided to take the next steps. Milorad suggested that it would be best to clarify whether these assumptions could be confirmed with a DNA test. At the beginning of April, Natalija sent her saliva samples to the German institute. We waited anxiously for the result. On the 10th of April 2012 we received the answer; which was a bit devastating for me.

There was only a 16% likelihood that Natalija was my half sister and therefore Radojica my father. To be on the safe side, we decided to take another test with Branislava. For this test, the two sisters invited me to visit Belgrade. We agreed to meet at the beginning of May and I made my way to Belgrade to spend three days getting to know the home and family of my supposed father.

In anticipation: these were to be the most beautiful and exciting days that I experienced during this time.

I was a guest of Branislava's family (including her husband Dragan and sons Aleksa and Janko). Everyone had prepared for my visit. At first Milorad interpreted, all other days English dominated, but from time to time German was spoken when Ana Matic, a distant relative, came to visit. I also met the family of Natalija (her husband Miloje and children Kosta, Ivan and Nina). The warm Serbian hospitality was always in the foreground.

After an exciting day in Belgrade, we sat together for a few hours late into the evening, photo albums were rolled over and memories of their father (who died in 1996) were unearthed.

Milorad, Natalija, Branislava greeted me at the Belgrade airport

The daughters idolized their father Radojica, and he had always been on a fairly high pedestal. Therefore, this sentence was in the room: "Radojica would never have done such a thing!" They just could not imagine that he had a son in Germany, that he never mentioned him and did not care about him.

Nevertheless, the sisters recognized my supposed features on Radojica's youth photos; and they concluded that my character would be very similar to their

Radojica's grave in Belgrade

father's. One day we visited the final resting place of Radojica and laid down flowers. Branislava and Natalija left me alone at the grave for a while. I'll be honest, I cried like a castle dog. It was one of the most moving moments in my life. I was convinced I had found my father. The families of Branislava and Natalija did everything to give these three days validation. Very often we dealt with the Serbian history and during a city tour a piece of the past came to life again; especially through the remaining ruins of 1941, 1944 and 1999.

On 6-7 April 1941, Belgrade was destroyed by German bombers (tens of thousands dead), on 16/17 April 1944 by the US Air Force and the Royal Air Force (1,200 dead). and 1999 from March to June by NATO (with thousands of deaths).

Ruins in Belgrade

I served as a Bundeswehr soldier in Kosovo in 1999/2000 and 2004 and was reluctant to enter into this discussion, because I knew about the particularly hostile relations between the Serbs and the Albanians (Kosovars). But when I told them that we also protected the Serbs in Prizren (e.g., a Serbian monastery, the priest wanted to lynch the Albanian mob, but our local unit was able to prevent it), they became somewhat calm.

These three eventful days came to a rapid end. Gifts were given to each other with the promise to see each other as soon as possible. I received some photos from Radojica's album. The most important was a small group photo of 28 Serb prisoners of war in Kühnhaide. It is still very valuable to me.

I sent Branislava's saliva test immediately to the Galantos Institute after my return. The result came three weeks later; unfortunately again the results were negative. The probability was only about 6% that we were related. I suspected that something was wrong, because there was nothing wrong with the chain of evidence from Kühnhaide. Based on my suspicions, I was able to convince both of them to do another Y-chromosome test with George, a son of Radojica's half-brother. That test would be conclusive if George was a direct male descendant!

The comparison of 11 positions resulted in only 3 matches; but to clearly identify Radojica's relationship or paternity all 11 of them had to match in order. Now it was imminently clear to me and everyone involved that Radojica could not be my father. The disappointment spread to everyone.

During this time, the managing director of Galantos Genetics in Mainz, Mr. Schatzl became quite friendly. His colleagues, Dr.Schacker and Dr.Siebert, were also fascinated by my story. Because my case was so unique, his other employees became interested in these results as well. Because these tests were rather expensive, the managing director decided that all future tests conducted under my identification were to be given a discount.

Suddenly, Mr Schatzl surprised me by suggesting that my data (Y chromosomes) should be compared to an international database. There were two outstanding results. The first significant finding was that I belong to the haplotypes of the Balkans and therefore have Serbian roots. This was a very important clue for my further research. The second showed that almost the same Y chromosomes were found in a man in Italy. Although I had previously identified this similarity, I had not received any information from the Italian authorities. Mr. Schatzl then told me that this ancestor lived a few hundred years before my time and that the match was not complete.

Initially, I put my Belgrade experience on paper and several local newspapers reported on it. Additionally, the many photos were publicized, for example the little photo depicting the 28 Serbs in Kühnhaide. As our investigations progressed, this historical photograph, which came from the winter of 1941/42, became the major basis of our work.

Prior to the newspaper publication we began to believe that further research would be very difficult. My Kühnhaider and Zwönitzer friends had run out of options, and I came close to stopping the search for my father.

I had several significant realizations: Rudolf could not be my biological father; because I was the child of a Serbian. First and foremost my wife encouraged me to continue. She knew that I would not get inner peace unless I had my paternity question answered. I would have liked to have known with whom my mother Frida had a liaison, in the middle of the war. Additionally, her family protected that knowledge. It must have been a very special person for whom she risked her life, for such circumstances were severely punished at that time if they were exposed. Would I ever find out? Why did Frida and Rudolf take this secret to their graves?

There was another glimmer of hope again in the summer of 2012, when I made contact with the Serbian newspaper "Blic" and its journalists Maja Anastasjevic and Svetlana Palic. Both soon became real friends and made a significant contribution to the success of publishing the articles and photos about me and finding my dad. Also the local Saxony editorial offices worked on this topic:

A newspaper clipping from the Serbian newspaper "Blic"

Wolfgang Petzolds Suche nach seinem Vater geht weiter

Der Kölnhändler hat die Familie eines einstigen verblichenen Kriegsgefangenen besucht. Doch dessen Sohn ist er wohl nicht.

34

After several articles were published, Serbian journalists received more than 300 letters, e-mails and telephone conversations with people who were related to prisoners of war in Germany.

On the Internet, generally positive comments were published about the well-known liaison of a Serb with a German and the more than 70 year search. Many people wanted to help. It must not be forgotten, however, that negative statements did appear, on the Serbian as well as on the German side. I spared myself the details here. It made me think that some people did not learn anything from history. About 25 of the most important and promising inquiries were sent to me.

The first contact I received was from a family named Jovanovic from Sevojno near Uzice, who has become extremely involved in the search for my father. We became good friends.

Sandra, Miroslav, Ankica, Alexandar and in front Mother Kose (73)

For a better understanding, here is the group photo of the Serbs, numbered, as a result of my long research:

Name assignment of 18 persons: Group photo - previously identified persons

1 Jovanovic, Vlastimir, Stepojevac near Belgrade, * 1901 + 1993, with farmer Mueller, Mrs. Danica

2 Vrancevic, Vojislav * 1913 + 1967 Stepojevac near Belgrade, near farmer Oskar Hennig

3 Boskovic, Vitomir Stepojevac, * 1907 + 1993 at Belgrade, with farmer Hübner

4 Simic, Slavaljub * March 26, 1919 + October 7, 2002, with the farmers Groß, Fankhänel, Hübner, Willy Neukirchner and Lessmüller in Lenkersdorf

5 Veljovic, Bozidar

6 Djurdjevic, Jordan * 15.01.1915 in Carina

7 Miljkovic, Radojica * 1.11.1919 + 1996 Belgrade, with farmer Bruno Hennig

8 Aleksic, Milan - At Bauer Paul Neukirchner with Velizar Colic

9 Precanica, Milan * April 23, 1913 in Bakuga, + 1990, father Nikola

10 Jovanivic, Zivko * 16.3.1916 Krusevac, Bivolje 230

11 Colic, Velizar * 1914 Sevojno, + 2006, at farmer Paul Neukirchner

12 Mitrovic, Miodrag at farmer Bach - KZ !!!

13 Bakovlev, Petar, born April 21, 1919 in Velika Kikinda

14 Micic, Milenko * 1905 from Stepojevac

15 Nikolic, Rrvoslav, born April 21, 1920 in Belgrade

16 Rajevac, Radomir, born May 21, 1888 in Otanj

17 Kekez, Jovan, born December 28, 1909 in Mokrin

18 Marinkovic, Milan, * 1909 in Uramcica Posowska

I will come back to some of them in the course of my presentation. Their destinies will accompany me in their search for my identity. Ultimately, they showed me the way to my father's successful final determination.

Velizar Colic

Due to the intensive contact with the family Alexander and Ankica Jovanovic we found out that Kose's father, Velizar Colic (No. 11 in the group photo) also was kept captive in Kühnhaide. He is said to have told the family shortly before his death that he had had a son in Kühnhaide. Immediately, I was sent photos of Velizar. There was a certain resemblance to me.

Now I know that this family Jovanovic wanted to welcome me into their family; because above all, Kose would have found a brother.

Velizar Colic

his wife Stanimirka with daughter Kose.

So the search started again. In addition, I had intensive discussions with my friends in Kühnhaide, especially with Hellmut Kuntz. Even though he was 81 years old, he was still able to tell many stories about the prisoners. At the end of the war, he was a 14-year-old boy who spent almost all of his spare time with the Serbs. Since the old " Volkssturmwachmänner" (old people's storm guards) knew him, the task of leading the prisoners to work and back to the accommodation was often assigned to Hellmut.

In fact, in the last year of the war, the Serbs had relative freedom. Some even stayed with the farmer they worked for. Now it was understandable how intimate relations with German women could have arisen. Hellmut reflected that he was often in Velizar's company who taught him a lot. For example, Velizar had found a worn out pistol (unusable for shooting). With this weapon, Hellmut and Velizar practiced the disassembly and assembly of the pistol.

In the summer of 2012, a lively e-mail exchange was concluded with the Jovanovics in Serbia. Hardly a week went by when we didn't have contact.
So I decided to do another DNA test between Velizar's daughter Kose and me. In mid-September 2012, the Kose's saliva sample results arrived in Mainz, almost at the same time as mine. Unfortunately, with a probability of 99%, this sibling test proved that I'm not the brother of Kose. Everyone was very disappointed, because we would have liked to be related.
They continued to support me in my search, but made me promise to continue searching for a brother of Kose in Kühnhaide. During the following visits to this place and the neighboring villages, I always had to consider at least two options: my past and that of Velizar and Kose.

What extensive, indeed almost scientific, activity was involved! In a recent report on April 24, 2013 to the Jovanovic family, I summed up and outlined all the stages of the search once more.

Final report regarding research on the descendants of Velizar Colic in the German war prison in Kühnhaide / Zwönitz from 1941 to 1945

On August 2nd, 2012, Alexandar Jovanovic wrote to me that his grandfather Velizar Colic (1914 to 2006) confided to his family at the end of his life that he had a son together with the daughter of Paul Neukirchner, who was born around 1944. In addition, Velizar's daughter, Kose, remembered a photo of two women and a blond boy (around 3-4 years old). The back said, "Come back, my heart!" This photo was taken by Velizar's wife, Stanimirka, after his return from captivity.

Searches performed:

1. The farmer Paul Neukirchner

From 1941 to 1945, Velizar Colic worked for the farmer Paul Neukirchner in Kühnhaide / Zwönitz, Kreis Aue, Chemnitz district.

At the time, Mr. Hellmut Kuntz was about 14 years old and could still remember Velizar well.

He said, "Velizar was a very kind, hardworking, and decent man. He was nice to the children." He went on to explain that the farmer Paul and his wife Lony were about 33 years old, at the time. They had six daughters, who were very young; the oldest was 13 years old. Velizar had a very good and family relationship with the whole family. The child that Velizar fathered, he must have had with another woman, because the daughters of Paul Neukirchner were out of the question because of their age. Based on Mr. Kuntz's statement, I had to keep looking.

2. The other farmer Paul Neukirchner (not related to the Paul Neukirchner under 1.)

This farmer had a daughter Ilse and a son Ernst. Ilse had a relationship with the Serbian prisoner of war Zivko Jovanovic

Zivko Jovanovic

(sergeant and superior of the 28 prisoners in Kühnhaide) and on the 8th of September 1943 gave birth to a daughter, Anneliese.
Zivko worked until the end of the war (May 1945) with this farmer. He recognized this child as his own and wanted to return to Germany to Ilse Neukirchner. They had contact until 1947, but then stopped.

Because Zivko and Ilse had an identified relationship, it can be ruled out that Velizar had a child with Ilse.

*Because of **Paul Neukirchner's (#1) daughter's** age 3, it is therefore improbable that the statement "he had a boy" with her was likely.*
However, based on the photos found by Anneliese Neukirchner/Tzscharke, I discovered that Ilse Neukirchner had a friend, Leni Gebhard, who was employed by the farmer Günther as a maid. This Leni could have been the other woman in the photo, because I suspected that Zivko and Velizar were also friends.

*That's why the search was done by the **family of 3. Leni Gebhard***

I had conversations with the still living members of the family, which ruled out that Leni Gebhard had a child with Velizar. This was confirmed to me by Christa Gebhard (sister-in-law of Leni, still living in the same house) and Reiner Jähn, son of Leni, born in 1948.

Further research:
*Because the investigations stagnated, I talked again with living people in Kühnhaide. Specifically, **all persons included under point 1 (Paul Neukirchner).***
During this further research, a daughter of Paul Neukirchner, Annelies Becher (78), residing in Dittersdorf, made some very interesting statements to me. She knew that the Kirsch family lived right next to Paul Neukirchner's farm and they also had close contacts with the farmer Neukirchner.

4. Elsbeth Koelke (née Kirsch) and Lotte Neukirchner (née Kirsch),
Regarding Elsbeth Koelke:

Knowing that Elsbeth's husband Erich was away for the entire war and did not come home until 1946, I suspected that the child in the photo Kose had seen could have been Peter (Sept 20, 1943). This assumption was confirmed by the fact that Elsbeth had taken her life in 1956. Only the DNA test with Peter and Kose provided the certainty that Peter could not have been the son of Velizar.

*Regarding **Lotte Neukirchner:***

Lotte was married to Willy Neukirchner (brother of Paul Neukirchner). He died in the war in 1942. Lotte had born a son in 1937.

According to statements by Annelies Becher (second oldest surviving daughter of Paul and Lony Neukirchner, née Kirsch), Velizar Colic had been around for years (about 1943- 1945) and had a close intimate relationship with Lotte Neukirchner. She also confirmed to me several times that she could not have had another child.

Annelies Becher reassured me several times that Velizar did not want to return to Serbia after the end of the war. But after he had been forced to do so, he later wanted to return to Lotte in Kühnhaide, but this did not happen. From today's point of view, this is conditioned by the political situation in Yugoslavia (as well as in the Soviet Union). They were not allowed to go back. Even letters to Lotte had failed.

I have conducted several surveys, including the son of Lotte. Since he was a small boy at the time, it is understandable that he knew nothing about Velizar.

Since my interviews and research were unsuccessful, I extended the search and asked a total of 11 local institutions in the area for help (registry offices, archives, hospitals and parishes in Zwönitz, Aue, Lößnitz, Stollberg and Chemnitz). But even this research did not prove that Velizar had a child with a "Frau Neukirchner." However, prisoner Seaman Slavoljub Simic (1919-2002), who was arrested, reported in a statement to his mother that the Serbian prisoners were hiding a small child. When and where exactly this happened and who the father and mother were, cannot be reconstructed.

Conclusions:

According to previous findings, no proof can be provided that Velizar Colic had a biological child. However, this research indicates that Velizar had a close relationship with Lotte Neukirchner from about 1943 until the end of the war. In all likelihood, no child was born from this relationship. The chances of Velizar having a child with Lony Neukirchner (then about 33 years old, wife of farmer Paul Neukirchner, mother of six children where Velizar worked) are unlikely. All respondents vehemently refuted this thesis.

The assumption is obvious that Velizar did not have any biological children with a German woman. Lotte's son, who was about 7 years old at the end of the war, wanted to start a family and wanted confirmation of his paternity.
For the record:
Wolfgang Petzold

In this report, I tried to give the Jovanovic family a glimpse of how difficult it is, after so many years, to provide clear evidence, based on conjecture, circumstantial evidence and which children were born in those years. The records of Velizar Colic filled at least two files. I have not given up the search for the son of Velizar Colic and later in Kühnhaide again conducted extensive interviews of survivors.

Following the publication of the group photo in Serbia, the **Zivotic** family from Belgrade contacted me. It was another milestone on the trail of success. The father of Slavica, **Matrose Slavoljub Simic** (who died in 2002, No.4 in photo), had in his estate, photos of many prisoners and

a roll list of 20 men with rank and prisoner number. This list was sent to me by the Zivotics along with many memories from Slavoljub about Kühnhaide. For example, he told his children that they had been hiding a child of a prisoner of war for a long time with the farmer Neukirchner.

In one of her articles, the journalist, Mrs. Muth, published this photo in the Stollberger Zeitung and asked for help. Unfortunately, no one responded to the request. I have not found this child yet. Whether it came from Velizar Colic, could not be determined. There was no one in Kühnhaide who could give me a hint. I wonder why? That time had to remain top secret, because otherwise all the people involved would have been put against the wall or taken to

Is this the hidden child ?

the concentration camp. There were many examples. Prisoner-of-war children are still a topic of <u>taboo</u> in society, also because even today, after so many years, nobody is intensively involved in it. The pictured list had Slavoljub Simic at the end of the war with him. How he obtained it, one can only guess. Nobody has given him this.

Name list of the commanding officer of the Serbian prisoners, Uffz. Göckeritz

№	Name	Vorname	Kgf. Nr.	Dienstgrad	
1	Jovanović	Zivko	84216	Feldwebel u.	Vertrauensmann
2	Precanica	Milan	83117	" "	
3	Rajevac	Radomir	80066	" "	
4	Djurdjević	Jordan	83705	Uffz.	
5	Colić	Velizar	82892	"	
6	Aleksić	Milan	83392	Ob-Waar	
7	Simić	Slavoljub	83391	" "	
8	Bakovljev	Petar	83010	Gefr.	
9	Vrancević	Vojislav	3602	Soldat	
10	Bosković	Vitomir	3599	"	
11	Datić	Zarko	4640	"	
12	Rackov	Pera	84417	"	
13	Topolić	Pojko	79760	"	
14	Popov	Nikola	94141	"	
15	Jovanović	Vaso	85818	"	
16	Jovanović	Vlastimir	2256	"	
17	Misić	Milenko	5607	"	
18	Milković	Radojica	83779	"	
19	Miladinović	Milorad	84930	"	
20	Bahar	Aron	82291	"	

I still maintain close contact with the Zivotic family from Belgrade today.

So far, a total of 5 DNA tests had been done to identify my Serbian father; all so far unsuccessful. But the only certainty was: "I am a Serb!"

So how do you proceed? Simply giving up was certainly not up for debate. Nevertheless, it was increasingly difficult to find more witnesses in Kühnhaide. My friends there did a good job, but we also found inexplicably a lot of rejection. The main tenor was: "Let the dead rest, we do not want to talk in the village!" These statements made me very sad. How can you still have such outdated views after more than 70 years?

But we had another iron in the fire. On the basis of the publication of the article and the group photo in "Blic" a **Mr. Dragan Vrancevic** from Stepojevac contacted me. He related information about his father:

Vojislav Vrancevic (No. 2, died 1967)

Another three soldiers (Vlastimir Jovanovic, Vitomir Boskovic and Milenko Micic, Nos. 1, 3 and 14) from this village were imprisoned together and all four can be seen in the group photo. He was convinced that his father Vojislav was also my father. We were in contact every day (he spoke good German) until Mr. Vrancevic was hospitalized. His sons Dejan and Slobodan helped us in his place.

Dejan was very well acquainted with the situation in the village of Stepojevac (he was also fluent in gossip). He then gave me an important and promising tip in December 2012.

Dragan Vrancevic, son of Vojislav Vrancevic

Dejan Vrancevic with family

After Dragan returned from the hospital, he and I wanted to have the DNA test. He was completely sure that I was the child of his father Vojislav. At the beginning of the sixties, he repeatedly indicated that he, too, could have had a child in Germany.

As Dragan's hospitalization extended, I could not wait any longer, but still wanted to continue my search. Now my wife and I took a closer look at the photo of the 28 prisoners. Many were actually out of the question. But number 1 in the photo seemed like a cut-out of my face.

Vlastimir Jovanovic (died 1993)

Why had we not noticed it before? Certainly we had not considered that many of the prisoners. But now, when we examined the images more closely (nose, eyes, face bones, chin, expression, etc.).

Vlastimir seemed to be a cookie cutter image of when I was that age, especially the mischievous smile which I could only have from him. Now the search was intensive towards Vlastimir Jovanovic. Our friendly family Jovanovic (who is not related to Vlastimir's family) found out that three of Vlastimir's daughters were still alive. The youngest, Vuka Solaja, lives in Belgrade. Again, we were optimistic that I finally found my dad. There followed an intensive exchange of correspondence with Vuka. Here are some excerpts from our correspondence:

Vlastimir compared to me (above) and below Jovanovic, Vrancevic, Misic and Boskovic (right)

First mail from Vukosava Solaja - 01.11.2012 Hello Wolfgang,
I was pleasantly surprised to learn that we could easily have another brother. I would be glad if it were true, and if not, I am honored to have helped that person to know the truth about his background.
I know that my father worked on the farm for a family that had only words of praise for him.
My father was born on 14.10.1901. Father Cosma and mother Katherine were teachers in Stepojevc. My father and mother Danica got married in 1924. They had six children:
1 Olga - 4.9.1925 - 20.06.1998
2 Veselin - 06.02.1928 - 02.12.2000
3 Ruzica -12.09.1930
4 Dusan - 08.05.1933 -31.05.2012
5 Leposava -18.02.1947
6 Vukosava - 08.09.1950
As you can see the rest of us, and all three, we are ready to help you. Looking at the pictures, we are convinced that you have a lot of similarities with our dad and your son in the plaid shirt (Robbi) too. Maybe this is enough to start with and surely we will continue to serve.
Best regards to you and your family

Address: Šolaja Vukosava ul Nastic 2, 11 132 Belgrade

I sent my existing test results to a Belgrade institute, along with your saliva samples, Vuka. After two days, on 09.11.2012, we received the result. Again negative !!

I was just desperate. Again my wife straightened me out and came up with the idea of once again writing to the International Red Cross in Geneva. Previously, I had received results from my inquiries via e-mail.

With the list of names from the estate of Slavoljub Simic (see the group photograph with the 18 identified Serbian POWs) as an attachment, I simply sent another e-mail with a request to investigate the names we had not requested previously.

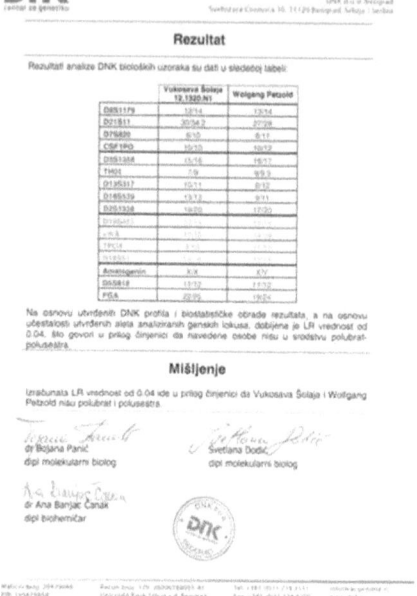

I did not hope for much, but I was mistaken!

After just one week, I received in the mail a thick A-4 envelope with more than 50 sheets of identifying information about the 15 Serbian prisoners in Kühnhaide. I could not quite grasp the fact that the Red Cross in Geneva had provided these documents on such short notice, without any bureaucratic hurdles, and at no cost! They wished me much success in their cover letter about my searching for my father. Obviously, they knew my story exactly.

I compiled a roll-call list of all remaining prisoners, with all the facts that were available (date of birth, place, ID number, etc.).

At the beginning of December I sent this list to my helpful family Jovanovic in Sevojno. I suggested that they should only explore the possibility of making contact with some offspring of these soldiers.

The very next day, they reported that they had already questioned 6 people (families) who were shortlisted. The next one was actually the only one that looked promising:

Milan Precanica (# 9, died 1990)
He told his family he had also worked for the farmer Hennig and that my mother Frida had been "crazy about him" (this was certainly the one who was confused with Radojica.). I wanted to pursue this "hot tip".

We found his descendants in Croatia. We learned that they lived in a small village called Gornja Bacuga and were deported from Serbia after the Croatian-Serbian war (1991-1995). I also received a lot of historical background information. After this war, the official Croatian public statement was: "One third of the Serbs were liquidated, one third of them emigrated, and one third of them integrated into Croatian society!"

Once again it was my dear Jovanovic family who made contact with the relatives who immigrated to Germany in the 1960s (Rada Weissenberger). These in turn arranged contact with Stojan, a son of Milan, who was still living in Belgrade and was ready for a DNA test.

Fortunately, another male relative lived in the Black Forest, and I was able to shorten the tedious procedure and obtain a Y chromosome test from Vaso Precanica (a son of Milan's brother). Again, this test (it was the eighth) turned out to be negative!

Rada and brother Stojan Precanica (around 1976)

Milan Precanica (left) and
Jordan Djurdjevic

However, this setback also had a positive side. Notably, since that test I have found friends and colleagues with the Rada family and Lothar Weissenberger and secondly, we found the actual son of Milan Precanica through many conversations in Kühnhaide. It was R. Milan B. and therefore Stojan was his brother. His mother had given him the second name Milan, after the war registry was created.

Chapter 4.3. - Finally found my new Boskovic family

But while the test with Vaso was underway, an urgent e-mail came from the Jovanovics. They had found a family, Boskovic in Stepojevac,
They were told that their father, grandfather and great-grandfather **Vitomir Boskovic (No. 3)** was also in Kühnhaide and had two children (boys) there with two different women. He is said to have confessed that to his wife after his return from the war. As it turned out, before his capture on April 7, 1941 in Belgrade, he already had 5 children with his wife Andelija (died 1989).

Andelija and grandmother Spasenija with 5 children (picture taken around 1937)

The five children of Vitomir, from the left Milka, Olivera, Milunka, Vojislav and Milena

It was a stroke of luck! The Boskovic family was very cooperative and emailed news and photos about the Jovanovic family on December 9, 2012, with an attachment photo of a farmer's wife, where Vitomir had worked. An immediate plea in Kühnhaide revealed that the person in the photo was a Mrs. Hübner. (Later we learned that a late son of Mrs. Hübner had corresponded with Vitomir in the '70s. The son sent photos of himself and the family to Vitomir, and we believe that Karl Hübner was the other German son of Vitomir, but we cannot prove it.) Although I knew that my parents were friends

49

with the Hübners and my mother had occasionally helped out on the farm, I still could not find any reference to my problem. One day later we received another e-mail with an unknown photo of my mother Frida. It had been found in the estate of Vitomir.

Then, on December 15, 2012, the absolute breakthrough: A photo of me at the age of about 9 months was discovered at the Boskovics in an old metal box, hidden in the attic. When they sent it to us by e-mail, we were celebrating the 13th birthday of our granddaughter Nathalie. We had a grand celebration for both occasions.

Later it was said that Vitomir's wife Andelija had destroyed everything Vitomir had brought back from captivity, but in all probability grandmother Spasenja (died 1968) was able to save the two photos for posterity, luckily! There was no doubt that Frida had given him these two photos when he left Vitomir in May 1945. The spell was broken. We were on the home stretch!

Hanni Hübner   Mother Frida   Me

By now I had telephone contact with the Boskovic family, later on Skype, mostly in English, Russian and Serbo-Croatian. The translation was done via "google-translation" on the internet.

I initially had contact with many family members: the son of Vitomir, Vojislav (82), his son Dragan (42), his wife Ljiljana (39), daughter Milica (16) and son Mark (9). More photos and documents found their way to Dresden and back to Stepojevac. Everyone knew that we had reached our goal and I had found my father Vitomir Boskovic and his family. The chain of evidence was finalized. The photos, the fact that Frida had worked with Vitomir with the brewer Hübner, and also the testimony of my Kühnhaide witnesses corroborated these facts. What an exciting moment.! The Boskovic family was fully aware that I was the son of Vitomir. The characteristics of both of us were subjected to an "investigation" via the Internet. Everything checked out - I was almost a "Boskovic".

Nevertheless, based on past experience, we decided to perform the DNA test. The safest thing was to pinpoint the identity of the Y chromosomes of the male line. For this I sent my previous test results to the Belgrade Institute and Vojislav gave his samples on December 28, 2012 from there. On New Year's Eve, December 31,2012 around 4:00 pm, my wife called me into the house from the garden (I had just fed our many cats) and read me a message. When I heard the short content of this e-mail, written by Milica Boskovic, I went into a total "breakout" for a moment and shouted out all the pent-up tension: "Yeah, yaa ...!". It was done and like a miracle! The text contained only three words in large letters:

Vitomir + Frida = Wolfgang

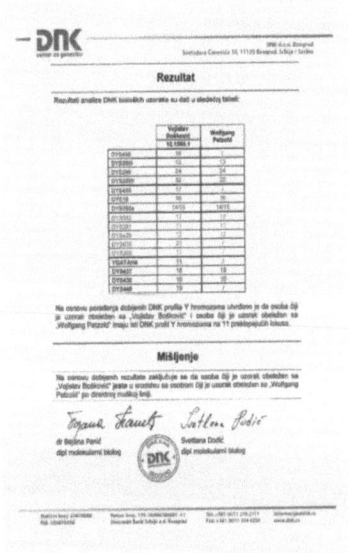

The front page result of Vojislav's DNA test

Result of the test

51

Of the 11 positions tested, all were identical. I found my father and my new Boskovic family. At that moment, I was the luckiest person on earth.

My father Vitomir as a young soldier

Soldbook* by Vitomir Boskovic
* http://www.panzeraufgd.co.uk/soldbuch1.html

We used the coming weeks to intensively exchange information about our families and immediately planned the first meeting in Serbia. All of the Boskovic family members gathered memories, old documents and photos. A plethora of names, birth dates, places, relationships, and so on, were exchanged over the internet. Finally, I had a cache of about 40 people. There was nothing left for me to do, but sort everything in a table

To sum up: It helps a lot to know a bit about the structure of the family. Here is an excerpt from it:

Olivera (died 2009) - my sister
Slobodan * 1950 Dobrosav * 1953
Predrag * 1975 Ivan * 1978
Duzan * 2000

Milunka (2002) - my sister
Radoslav (1954) Ranka (1962)

Milos (1984) Marja (1989)   Ivana (1984) Mladena (1987)
oo Marija   oo Miroslav.

Nina (2012)   Andrea   Aleks
Lena (2012)   (2010)   (2012)

Vojislav (age 80) - my brother
Duzanka (1970)
Zeljiko (1966)
John (18)
Dragan (1972)
Ljiljana (1975)
Milica (14)
Mark (8)

Milena (75) - my sister
Daca (1970)
Maja (1976)
Miljan
Andrej (9)
Andjelko (8)

Milka (75) - my sister
Marijana (1961)
Aleksandar (1955)
Igor (30)
Filip (28)
Gordana (1964)
Dragoljub (1955)
Aleksandar (22)

To be honest; even today I have to think about who belongs to whom; all the names are not always immediately available to me. But that was the smallest problem.

Meanwhile, I tried to find out more about other "Serbs' children" in Kühnhaide. According to prudent estimates, there must have been between 10 and 20 children, based on the knowledge of descendants and grandchildren of some Serbs. In the photo "Haymaking" it becomes clear why the prisoners had " "einen Stein im Brett " (a stone in the board) for the women.

His own men were at war or had fallen. It was reported that the Serbs had a very industrious and obliging nature. Often they represented the "replacement head" in the peasant families. They ate at the table (when officials came, they were quickly shipped to another room) and organized much of the work on the farms and fields. They had been housed centrally in a former stable, which they did not always use as accommodation. At the end of the war, they often spent the night in the barns or in the stable.

In all the media in which my story was published, I have always stressed that I have no grudge or other negative feelings, but I am full of respect for the men and women who lived in such dire times, and I bow before your humanity! Only my mother has to accept my reproach that she never managed to tell me the truth. At the latest, after the death of my father Rudolf in 1984, she could have done so. My father Vitomir was still alive at that time (until 1993). As an officer of the NVA I would certainly have had the chance to travel to the former Yugoslavia to get to know my father and his family, for those who had an intact family were allowed such trips.

Some thoughts on my parents:

With hindsight, after almost 70 years and knowledge of this story, I can look at some of my childhood and youth life situations from a different angle. I often wondered why my mother was so nervous, even though I saw no reason for it. Today I know that the trigger in this mystery was the truth about my ancestry, the secret which my parents kept for a lifetime and took to the grave. Only now can I remember how my mother made several suicide attempts in the early fifties. At that time I had experienced such situations as a child of 7 years up close. But only four years ago, while researching my first book, all the terrible memories came back.

I grew up very sheltered, but now I can interpret situations in my life that are probably causally related to Viton and my mother Frida's liaison. Why, for example did my father never hug me or respond to strict "little pranks"? The question of why Rudolf did not leave my mother at that time is relatively easy to answer. In the era of National Socialism, this love would have been punished as a crime, and a separation would have revealed everything.

There are also examples in Kühnhaide and the surrounding area where those involved were shot or sent to a concentration camp. Hellmut Kunz told me such a story that stunned me. Miodrag Mitrovic(number 12 in the Photo.) worked for the farmer Bach The Serbian prisoners received care packages from the Red Cross (from England and the USA), and the young girls and boys were keen on the "content" of the packages. Chocolate and chewing gum were for many foreign words at this time. A young 14-year-old girl had it out especially for Miodrag. Even though there was nothing to be distributed, she tried to "approach" him. Since Miodrag loved his wife and family at home in Serbia, he snubbed her every time, according to Helmut. All Helmut knew was that Miodrag suddenly disappeared. Much later it turned out that he had been

The third from the left is Miodrag

slandered with a false statement. The 14 year old girl had claimed that he raped her. It was a revenge accusation that might have cost him his life. It was suspected that Miodrag had been taken to a camp.

The girl disappeared after the war. A woman from Kühnhaide gave her name; and related that she lives somewhere in West Germany. She was probably driven from her home out of shame. During my research for my father, I also wanted to clarify the fate of Miodrag Mitrovic, but it fell by the wayside somehow. Maybe I'll catch up at some point and continue that search.

Tailor Arnold in Zwönitz at the market in winter 1944/1945

If I internalize this story, then in my eyes my father Rudolf is the real hero in my life! He had to have known about my mother's relationship with the Serbian Vitomir Boskovic. Nor can it be excluded that Radojica Miljkovic (Zeppelin) was closely involved with her. Zeppelin was transferred circa 1944 from the command in Kühnheide to Zwönitz for the tailor Arnold, on the presumption that he had to be taken out of the "line of fire". Maybe my father Rudolf had a hand in it. He knew many people in the village (from being around sports, as a carpenter, etc.)

In the spring of 2013 I was invited to Stepojevac for my first visit with my new family. The preparations in Serbia ran from January to April 2013 at full speed. There was a lot to organize. Especially my niece Marijana Djukanovic (age 52) from Belgrade, the Boskovics from Stepojevac as well as the journalists Maja Anastasievic and Svetlana Palic, all who were determined to make my stay in Serbia as pleasant as possible. Unfortunately, Ilse could not accompany me because someone had to be home with our four-legged friends. Instead she came up with the idea that I could fly to Belgrade with our boys Robert (age 50) and Sascha (age 42), especially since I had never traveled anywhere with them alone. We should have beautiful days in Serbia.

First visit to Serbia with my new Boskovic family

There are few suitable words that can even approximate my feelings that moved me after returning from Serbia. These six days were among the most beautiful and emotional in my life. I can rightly claim that I was born again.

I want to try to review the individual days, to give a small impression how I got to know my new family in Serbia.

In agreement with all the participants, the trip was scheduled for April 25-30, 2013. At the end of January, Ilse had booked the nights in the hotel "Konak Knezevina" in Vranic near Belgrade.

There were three beautiful individual rooms for Robert, Sascha and me. For each person the cost was 90 euros for 5 nights with breakfast. Coming from German cost of living standards, this price was peanuts. The distance to Belgrade is about 30 km and to Stepojevac 11 km. Immediately all flights were booked via Germanwings.

After they were informed of our travel itinerary, my new family started planning our stay. My niece Marijana felt the need to organize our stay from beginning to end and to be available as a companion. She proved to be truly talented and mastered this logistical challenge excellently. All family members were included, so that we could get to know their living environment.

Sascha, Robert and I at the Belgrade airport

Daca and Marijana welcome us at the airport

57

My dear family Boskovic in Stepojevac

My siblings and me in Stepojevac

My pretty nieces Duzanka, Marijana,
Maja and Daca

The grave of Vitomir and Andelija in Stepojevac

In Dresden, we had procured "small gifts" for the big new family, which had grown to more than 40 people. In the end, we had trouble stowing these "little things" in a large suitcase and a travel bag. I had to comply with customs regulations. Here is a small selection of our gifts:

Gift

Gift Bags

The "adventure" could begin!

The weather forecast for Greater Belgrade predicted temperatures of around 30 degrees Centigrade (86 degrees Fahrenheit) for our stay; And so it happened.

On the 25th of April we left the Dresden airport and landed in Belgrade at noon in the Serbian capital. My niece Marijana (52), her husband Alexandar (57), niece Daca (42), the journalists Svetlana Palic, Maja Anastasjevic (interpreter) of the magazine "Blic", a photojournalist and a driver from the newspaper were ready to pick us up. Immediately, we received first impressions of great hospitality. Everyone was kissed Serbian style. Good friends and family members are kissed three times on the cheek in Serbia. With three vehicles, we initially went to the hotel in Vranic to check in and repackage the presents. The hotel was waiting for other family members as well. For the first time, I was able to embrace my sister Milena (age 75), her daughter Maja (age 37) and Maja's husband Miljan (age 38). I will not soon forget that first contact with my sister. We were in our arms for a long time; Tears flowed on both sides. It was as if we had not seen each other for a long time.

Then at 2:00 pm a total of 13 people in four vehicles drove to Stepojevac, 11 km away, home of my father Vitomir and his family. My father's house is located far from the main road, and is only accessible by bumpy country lanes, but surrounded by beautiful green countryside. At the house, in the midst of meadows, trees, sheep, dogs, pigs and young geese, we welcomed about 20 other family members.

I remembered later what happened next. When we got out of the car and approached my father's family, I initially greeted my brother Vojislav (age 80) and my other sister Milka (age 75). She is the twin sister of Milena. Fate determined this outcome: I lost my sister (Inge) but acquired three new siblings.

One can only guess what was going on inside us at that moment. There were real emotional outbursts. I believe that my brother Vojislav was the most agitated. He just could not show it in the same way because of a chronic disease.

Then we were introduced in turn to all the other family members; all according to Serbian ritual. Afterwards, a welcome drink was served. They served home-made raki and for all non-alcoholic drinkers, soft drinks. Now everyone was looking for a seat under the trees in the garden and we immediately engaged in lively conversations. Since Maja Anastasjevic (my interpreter) and my niece Daca spoke

German, the greeting was uncomplicated. However, Maja was only present on the first day, Daca could not always be around us, so we agreed on English as the main communication. Marijana and Sasha were the best at expressing themselves. My language skills lagged behind, so that in my English conversation many Russian words appeared, but they were understood by most; of course, with great humor. This entire language confusion we called "Esperanto".

The big event of the day was yet to come: The visit to the grave of my father Vitomir. At around 6:00 pm we set off. They led us along narrow asphalt roads and dirt roads to the nearby "cemetery"; not comparable to our cemeteries. The tombs are located in the open field, surrounded by shrubs, trees and tall grass. The community gravestone of Vitomir and his wife Andelija is made of black marble and made a very positive impression. Surrounded by all the family members and the press, I laid down a beautiful bunch of flowers and a bouquet of flowers (both had been provided by the hotel). It was another emotional moment. The next day, I decided to go to the grave alone. A few rows away I laid flowers on the gravestone of Vitomir's mother, my grandmother Spasenija.

The celebration was continued at Vitomir's house. The circle of family and the guests sat down at a festive and plentiful table; the main guest (me) was always placed at the head. This is what happened on the following days during our visits. People talked, discussed and photographed a lot. A multilingual, oriental-sounding babble of voices always filled the room. The focus was always the fact that I had found my new family. Everyone was very happy.

I do not want to describe in detail what delicious treats and drinks were served. The whole thing lasted at least two hours. Maja and Svetlana ("Blic") had to say goodbye because a long working day was waiting for them on Friday. We separated like good old friends. I think good friends is what we became in the last few months, because of their tremendous help in finding my father.

Dragan (son of Vojislav), Ljiljana (his wife), Milica and Mark showed us the house, the yard and all the animals (sheep, pigs, young geese, two dogs that were always around us). Discussion groups, almost everyone with a glass or a tray full of goodies in their hands, were scattered around the house and in the garden. So the first day came to an end and we were driven to the hotel very late in the evening. Overjoyed but dog-tired, we fell into bed. We had experienced a hospitality that was indescribable. It was a great experience for me and my sons.

<u>Second day (April 26):</u>

At 09:00 o'clock, we had breakfast in the hotel (with all the bells and whistles), and a 10:00 o'clock departure for me (with Duzenka and her husband Zeljiko) to travel to Stepojevac to visit my brother. Marijana and Aca (Alexandar) came to take Robert and Sascha for a tour of Belgrade. In the late afternoon they too arrived tired but happy in Stepojevac.

Immediately after my arrival, I asked to visit my father's grave once more. All alone, I could now let my feelings run wild. It was a very moving moment for me. At lunchtime, the TV station "PRVA" (like ARD in Serbia) surprised us with an interview in Stepojevac. Although we did not know anything about it before, we just had to "put on a good face in the game" in the big bustle. It turned out to be an interesting time in which we were able to brush up on our English skills again (the Abitur* was exactly 50 years ago, linguistic class with English, Russian, Latin).
* Abitur is a qualification granted by university-preparatory schools in Germany, Lithuania, and Estonia. It is conferred on students who pass their final exams at the end of their secondary education, usually after twelve or thirteen years of schooling. https://en.wikipedia.org/wiki/Abitur

Again, I was taken to my father's grave for TV recordings. I made both English and German statements for airing on Serbian television in early May.

Milica, me, the director and Dragan

In the afternoon Milica, John, Dragan and I visited Milica and Mark's school. The director, the history teacher and the English teacher accompanied us through the schoolhouse. The glass showcase, in which Milica had exhibited historical pieces by Vitomir (identification tag, documents, etc.), was opened by the director so that I could photograph everything.

We arranged telephone contact with the English teacher on my return, for more details about the imprisonment of the four soldiers from Stepojevac. In exchange. The information could be used for history lessons.

We went to the 1912–1919 war memorial, where some Boskovics were memorialized. We then visited the Orthodox Church of Stepojevac, also a enjoyable experience. Incidentally, I found out in the church that the patron saint of the Family Boskovic is "Saint George" (hence mine).

Dragan in front of the
1912 – 1919 war memorial

Afterwards we strolled through the "inner city" past the home pub of my father Vitomir (many anecdotes were told). Ironically, I stumbled and fell lengthwise on the "nose". Of course, there was a big smile and everyone said, "Well, if that was not a hint from above!" Vitomir, Frida and Rudolf wanted to prevent me from going to the pub and teased me about skating on thin ice which is why everyone was laughing. Through woods and corridors we went back to the other waiting relatives.

Afterwards, we met with Vuka Solaja, the daughter of Vlastimir Jovanovic (one of my supposed fathers), in the farmstead of Dragan Vrancevic, about ten minutes away from the Boskovics. Unfortunately, we could only spend about an hour in their house and garden because the other family was expecting us back. Vuka is a wonderful woman from Belgrade who took a short walk with me to her father Vlastimir's house. She hugged and kissed me again and again. She would have liked to have been my sister. Actually, in such a situation I always feel quite anxious.

My patron saint "Saint George"

On this occasion I learned that Vlastimir Jovanovic in Kühnhaide had a relationship with a Maria Spicka (Polin) during his imprisonment. This was another interesting aspect of my Kühnhaide research. Later, I could not find a trace of her in Kühnhaide. Possibly because in addition to the Serbian prisoners, there were many foreign workers and later refugees who lived in the village.

The early evening was spent outdoors enjoying much food and drink. They tried to persuade us to stay overnight. Our argument, that we were leaving the next day, was ultimately stronger. However, we made a promise to come back as soon as possible, and in particular they wanted Ilse to be there. Especially Daca had put Ilse in her heart, despite the fact that she only knew her voice.

The farewell to Stepojevac was very tearful (no one was ashamed of these tears of joy). We were back at the hotel by 9:00 pm. The short "nightcap" in the hotel restaurant turned into a long evening full of emotions about the past hours. In addition, I had the opportunity to speak with my "boys" about many family things that they did not know before, especially about my negative experiences in my earlier years. They understood. I can say that this trip also helped us to strengthen our own family.

<u>Third day (April 27):</u>

The day was packed with many plans. First a visit to Milena's apartment in Belgrade (skyscraper); nice apartment, clean, age-appropriate, with children's room for the children of Maja (Andrej and Andjelko). Then my sister Milka and her boyfriend arranged for a meal in a restaurant where we spent pleasurable hours visiting. Sascha, Robert, Aca, Miljan and the two children Andrej (8) and Andjelko (9) watched the Belgrade Red Star football match. They became very enthusiastic, especially because of the stadium activities (fireworks, etc.). In the meantime, I visited with Marijana, Milena and Daca at the second house of Marijana in Obrenovac. Afterwards we went to Maja's (37, the youngest niece of mine) home. Maja and her husband's parents greeted us in a newly built house. Everywhere we were warmly received. Over coffee and cake, I once again presented my unbelievable story in English to all those present.

Everyone hung on to every word that came out of my mouth, Maya knelt in awe. At about 9 pm I accompanied Marijana on her way home to her apartment (an exclusive house on a hill in Belgrade). However, at that time Belgrade's traffic was so congested that it took us quite a long time to get there. We had lively conversation, toured the house and, of course, ate and drank. At midnight Ace took us back to the hotel. A quick nightcap and we quickly went to bed, because the next day was going to be very intense.

<u>Fourth day (April 28):</u>

We departed at 09:00 o'clock to Sevojno at Uzice, 150 km and 3 hours away from the hotel. We drove through beautiful scenery (low mountain range, 511 m above sea level) to the family of Sasa Jovanovic (grandson of Velizar Colic) and son of Kose (72) Jovanovic. On behalf of this family, I had started searching for the baby of Velizar in Kühnhaide.

It was a wonderful 5 hours with these extremely warm people. The return trip was a bit difficult due to battery damage in the car, but we were at the hotel around 8:30 pm and were able to review the past few days.

<u>Fifth day (April 29):</u>

In the morning we stopped in Stepojevac for just under two hours to say goodbye to everyone. As if magically conjured, journalists and cameramen from "VESTI" appeared (from the "Frankfurter General "). Consequently, our planned activities for the day were thrown off schedule The highlight of the morning was getting to know the twins Nina and Lena (15 months), the grandchildren of my deceased sister Milunka (died 2002) and the children of Milos and Marija.

I will probably remember the last farewell to my siblings forever. I just do not have the words to describe my feelings. My sons felt the same way. During this departure, I finally realized that I have now found my family in Serbia.

In the afternoon (3:00 pm) we were invited to Branislava (age 50) and Natalija Miljkovic's house in Belgrade for 3 hours. These are the daughters of Radojica Miljkovic, who was a friend of my mother and whose DNA tests were negative with mine. I had visited them in early 2012. When I was searching for my father, I became very connected to the Miljkovics and had maintained contact with them. These were hours of remembrance, rejoicing and friendship.

Daca picked us up at 6:00 pm at the Miljkovics and we then drove to Omoljica, where she lives with her partner Pavle (age 66). We had some raki and omelets and other goodies! Then she drove us back to the hotel. At 11:00 pm we had one last nightcap, and a brief review of the day. So our trip to Serbia came to an end.

Last day (April 30) - departure:

We planned to depart to the airport at 09:00 o'clock. We said goodbye to Marijana with a beautiful red rose bouquet arranged with ostrich feathers in appreciation of her "outstanding organizational and logistical masterpiece." She was a dear companion for these 5 days.

On the way to the airport, Aca, her husband, joined us. We sat down for another hour in a beautiful café, then said goodbye and went to the airport around 11:00 am. On the plane, each of us were lost in our own thoughts. We barely talked. The impressions from those days were so overwhelming that we were left speechless.

Conclusion:

For me, those days are unforgettable. I cannot express in words what I felt during my stay in Serbia with my new family. Let me use the words of the journalist Maja Anastasjevic, who wrote me an email after our return, to speak on my behalf:

"It was also a wonderful experience for me. I did not think that would affect me so deeply. It's just great that everything ended so well ".

And Daca, my niece, put it in a nutshell (original version):

"Our dear Wolfgang, our dear Ilsa, Robert and Sascha and families, Thank you for reporting that you arrived home. I'm so glad you're saying positive things about the new family.

Thank you from me and the whole family that you persisted in finding your roots, especially thank you for bringing so many sons into our family. From the first moment, I (Serbian) kissed you, I felt close to you. I am very glad that you have a desire to come back to Serbia. Immediately after your call today, I called my mother and conveyed your greetings. She said to greet you. She was at her neighbor's for coffee and talked about you, Robert and Sasa. In fact, her son lives in New York and saw videos on the internet about your life story, family Petzold and Boskovic.
He recognized my mother and responded immediately, and told others in New York to watch the video. So who knows how many people in the world have a similar fate, but few have the chance, will and perseverance to find the truth, and print a new page in his history book. Once again I thank you from my family for being in our lives.
I wish you all good health and good luck.
I kiss and I love the whole family.
Your Daca. "

These words of my niece Daca made me think, how very happy and confident I felt about seeing everyone again soon.

During our time in Serbia, further contacts with my relatives were announced. Marijana and her husband Alexandar were known for their tours as "globetrotters". Because of our invitation, they also planned to visit us in Dresden during their transit to Prague. With Robert's family, we decided to make their visit an experience too. At the end of July 2013, they arrived in Dresden on a Friday evening after a twelve-hour continuous car tour from Belgrade.

In the hotel "Academy", not far from our house, they moved into quarters. We then spent a wonderful evening together with us and in Robert's apartment. It was amazing how we could talk about many interesting family things in a relatively small circle. English, Russian and "gestures" were the predominant languages. In particular, our granddaughter Nathalie (13) stood out, who was now able to apply her language

In front of the hotel "Academy" with Marijana and Ace

skills practically. Late in the evening we drove Marijana and Ace back to the hotel.
It was heartwarming to greet and say goodbye. Of course, with the already well-known Serbian "3-times-kiss"!
Robert, Katrin and Nathalie showed them the cultural sights of

Nathalie and Marijana visiting the Zwinger

Dresden the next day. Despite the high temperatures, the "cultural program" was completed. The evening we spent together again in a Greek restaurant and in our garden.

Marijana, Ilse, myself and Alexandar

Dusk in our garden

Even though it was quite late, Ilse and I took our dear Serbs on a little tour through Dresden and the surrounding area. They loved how beautiful the city is at night, but they also loved the surrounding villages, with their forests and meadows.

The next day's tour was a little shorter. Robert's family went to Moritzburg with our visitors. Our Serbian relatives said that nature and architecture would be fascinating, ... and above all, very clean.
We then finished this day together in the Dresden "Brauhaus". The opportunity to learn more about the life and character of my father Vitomir was beneficial. Until she was thirty, Marijana knew him as an older man and she told some delicious episodes.

His grandchildren Duzanka, Dragan, Daca, Maya, Marijana, Gordana, Slobodan, Dobrosav, Radoslav and Ranka liked to be with him in Stepojevac, romping around with him on the farm,

Nathalie, Ilse and Marijana

driving with him in the horse-drawn carriage and the tractor. He was very fond of children and liked animals, mainly cats. He was a very hardworking person, on his legs from morning to night.

However, his wife Andelija never completely forgave him for the story about his activities during captivity. If he was ill, she would say the following: "Go to Frida in Germany and let her take care of you!"

Marijana also spoke of a small vice: After work, Vitomir often went to his local pub, which was 10 minutes away, drank a few beers and came back home a bit tipsy. She explained that was the custom at that time. Surely I had inherited the Serbian drinking genes from him as well.

The departure of Marijana and Aca was again very emotional. The time we spent with each other passed quickly.

In the spring of 2014, normality slowly returned to my life. For the past two years, I've been in a state of turmoil. Every day there were new insights that were accompanied by oversized emotions. It started early in the morning, when I "questioned" the internet and ended up late at night. I can say in all honesty that my life has new meaning.

Since my fate was not concealed to the public and the press, a number of people have contacted me. They had also been searching in vain for their fathers and were very interested in my advice and in sharing experiences.
(see chapter 5)

One might think that my story has now come to a decisive end. That's the way it is, but there are still questions about the German children of Velizar Colic, Vlastimir Jovanovic and some others. Anneliese's father, Zivko Jovanovic, is still the subject of my research. We want to know what happened to him. Zivko wanted to return to his girlfriend and daughter after the war. But we found out that this was forbidden in former Yugoslavia. Letters to the city administration in Krusevac have so far remained unanswered.
We succeeded in finding the son of Milan Precanica. A POW child also found the family of his French father.

We now have normal contact with most of our new Serbian relatives via telephone, Internet or Skype; news is exchanged, birthday greetings sent and reciprocated. We maintain consistent connections especially with our Serbian friends, the family of Sasa Jovanovic from Sevojno near Ucize. We enjoy Skyping or exchanging e-mails. Our two families are characterized by a commonality: love for animals and nature.
Worth mentioning is the following episode:

We presented to each other photos of our animals. In addition to dogs and cats, Jovanovics also had two beautiful white ducklings, which were inseparable.

Vitomir
Boskovic + Frida
Petzold

Frida and Vitomir at the Jovanovics in Sevojno

We suggested giving them the names "Frida" and "Vitomir" in memory of our story.

What a great idea! We were promised that both would not endure be the usual fate of poultry, but would be given special status and enjoy a long life. Ankica explained how affectionate they both are, and how it opens their hearts. They accompany "their owner" on their beer and vegetable plantation all day long and have become the darlings of the family.

At the beginning of 2015 Grandma "Spasenija" was added.

All three united. Front grandmother "Spasenija"

In the year 2008 we planted a maple tree in the foundling park Nochten for our grandchildren and attached a sign to it.

Our family tree in Nochten

Norway maple

Acer platanoide

For our grandchildren Nathalie, Ella, Sara – 2008
And our parents Irma and Ernst Schlutig
Frida and Rudolf Petzold
And Wolfgang's Serbian father Vitomir Boskovic
By Ilse and Wolfan Petzold - Dresden 2013

Since then, we have been going there every year and visiting our tree in this beautiful natural environment. In 2012/13 a completely new family situation arose for us, we decided to eternalize our parents on this sign. Now Ernst and Irma Schluttig, Frida and Rudolf Petzold and my father Vitomir Boskovic also found a place for eternity.

With the last photo before his death in 1993 I want to give my father Vitomir an honorable memory. He was already very ill.

"Dear Vitomir, I am grateful to you and to my mother Frida for having found each other, otherwise I would not exist. I am very sorry that we were not allowed to get to know each other. "

Vitomir's last photo

I had hoped that the successful search for my father Vitomir Boskovic would give me emotional closure after my first book Year 44 about my life. I wanted to leave behind all this extensive research, television reports and newspaper interviews in order to regain my inner peace. Now I know that this process does not work that way.

In my heart, I will always have more questions and desire more information. If others ask me for assistance, I cannot help but reflect on my own story. Above all, I think of the fundamental right of every person, that none of his or her historical roots should be withheld.

For this reason, I did not hesitate too long when MDR Broadcasting, Dresden approached me at the end of my search and invited me to record another TV interview in Kühnhaide. On the 13th of September 2013, we met for a whole day to record. Once again, it created an emotional climate for me, because I reviewed all the places where my father Vitomir worked, where he met with Frida and I was able to view for the first time, where I was probably conceived. All my friends from Kühnhaide and the surrounding area were present and they were able to contribute their thoughts as well.

Many thanks to you, dear Frieder Schneider (who had met the prisoners as a very small boy, they were housed in the stable of his house, but he unfortunately died in 2015), dear Helmut Simon and Hellmut Kuntz, dear Gisela, Anneliee, Andrea Hübner and all other friends. About 70 years ago, a

Presumably, I was born here, in the Hübner farm.

German-Serbian love began in this farmhouse (in the barn). After all these years, these buildings have hardly changed. A look into the interior of the barn gives one an idea of what must have happened then. It breathes a piece of history. I must have appeared very peculiarly. I cannot describe it. Certainly I had feelings of happiness and grief at the same time (heaven-high, saddened to death); I admit that my tears flowed.

On September 23rd, the three-minute interview was shown in MDR under the heading "Here from Four." It was a beautiful illustration of my incredible story. Since then, many people in my community have contacted me. All of them have helped me understand that my life has expressed something incredible, that there is really no explanation for many things in life, some things happen outside of our imagination; whatever it may be.

On the occasion of my father Vitomir Boskovic's 106th birthday, September 27, 2013, my wife and I invited everyone involved in the search for my dad to a meeting in Zwönitz / Kühnhaide. At the Café am Markt in Zwönitz, near Zeppelin's (Radojica Miljkovic) tailor Arnold's shop, we reviewed all the stages of our improbable search. It was a beautiful afternoon that ended with the promise for all of us to see each other again soon.

Zum 106.Geburtstag von Vitomir Boskovic

Since my book <u>Year 44</u> attained rather good sales figures by our standards (there were at least 350 in the 7 months of the year 2014), my wife and I have seriously considered in which media we could advertise our concerns, specifically breaking the taboos regarding "children of prisoners of war."

We cannot just accept that such an important issue is being forgotten. Once again, the *Sächsische Zeitung* (Saxon Newspaper) and the *Freie Presse* (Free Press) were the only ones who brought my story to the attention of the readers. We had to find ways to inspire television, filmmakers, directors, screenwriters, and so on about our idea. That's easier said than done.

We contacted known, lesser-known and unknown experts in the media industry. Everyone acknowledged that my story provided interesting information from which a documentary or feature film could be filmed. However, one statement by a documentary film director (I do not want to mention his name) illustrated one's status in this business. He said, "If you advance one million euros, you can think about such a project, unless you have a name in this industry!"

Nevertheless, in 2013 there were television recordings for the "Sachsenspiegel" from the MDR. This contribution of four minutes was shot by television journalist Ms. Römer-Menschel and her team here in Dresden Klotzsche. She reported on the preparation for my first trip to Serbia. I also tried to find a publisher in Serbia through journalists Maja Anastasjevic and Svetlana Palic. It was hopeless. Even her newspaper "blic" and the responsible Axel Springer publishing house withdrew from any consideration . Maja, who is an excellent interpreter, had translated the entire section (70 pages) into Serbian, completely free of charge.

During the Kühnhaide filming of the short MDR interview in September 2013, I became acquainted with the director Falko Schuster. With his "Newsdoc3GmbH" in Leipzig he shoots documentary films for MDR television. He recognized the potential of my subject matter and quickly registered with the MDR in Leipzig for the series "Unter uns," MDR-TV ("Below us").

MDR-TV "Below us"

Nobody really believed that I had a chance to participate in such a forum. Two weeks before the start of the program, which was to take place on November 28, 2014, in the second half of the evening, I received an invitation to be a guest at *Media City Leipzig* in Studio 3. The program would be recorded from 7:30pm to 9:30pm and then broadcasted at 10:00pm. If possible, I was asked to arrive around 4 pm with my own car, and then to have a run-through conducted at 5:30pm with everyone involved. The two presenters Axel Bulthaupt and Griseldis Wenner hosted a total of 8 speakers, who introduced themselves in the round.

I can remember that it was a very cold November day, and it gave me a unique experience. In my invitation, the driveway to the garage was outlined, but unfortunately it was closed that day for repairs. After circumnavigating the building several times, unnerved, I finally drove into a side street. Under the curious eyes of the local residents, I changed clothes on the street and immediately went to the studio. Since I arrived early, I was able to familiarize myself a little with the premises (studios, etc.). At around 4:00 pm, the guests were taken to the recording studio and assigned their seating places for the show. At that point, the cameras and microphones were placed in the appropriate position. Everyone had to speak a few sentences. Axel Bulthaupt talked to me a bit longer because he needed some background information. By that time, the atmosphere was positively tense, which, of course, increased even further until the taping began. Unfortunately, I had the misfortune to be the last interview, probably because I had been previewed frequently before the TV broadcast. Since they brought back an interviewee from a previous show, the moderators were under a time crunch and my interview was cut to about five minutes.

From my arrival to the studio until my contribution, for over five hours, I was in an exceptionally tense situation. By the time I completed my portion, the tension had manifested itself in my last sentences, and my voice was failing. Apparently, nobody noticed. I had meticulously prepared for the interview. Unfortunately, my contribution was edited and the actual broadcast was shortened. However, I believe that despite the circumstances, my story was appealing to the audience. At midnight all the participants met briefly in the canteen, but due to the advanced time and the physical exhaustion, we soon parted ways. Two weeks later I received a DVD of the broadcast. Many who saw the program, gave me a high marks and expressed regret that my portion was cut.

A relative sent me some photos of the broadcast:

Griseldis Wenner and Axel Bulthaupt talking to me   ... there was something to smile about

Even days after the broadcast, I have been contacted by many people. The basic theme, that it is the right of every human being to know his roots, has been well received. In some cases, however, I had to clear up the misconception that I earned a lot of money with my television appearances, newspaper articles, and book publications. For the record, my TV appearance paid me a fee of 200 euros plus travel costs, for every book sold I get 1.06 euros and for all newspaper articles I receive a free "thank you." But I must emphasize that the monetary reimbursement has little meaning for me, because my concern was and still is to give courage to other people who have experienced a similar fate.

... Pensive ...

When the television program aired, I was actually at the peak of my research. I had achieved almost everything I wanted, to find my father and Serbian family. Despite my successes, I have not given up the search for my supposed brother in Kühnhaide. I do not force that search because I can barely find anyone who could or would be able to provide information.

The first months of 2015 were marked by the preparations for the second visit to my Serbian family.

The second visit to my Serbian family

Meanwhile, several months had gone by again. The memories of my new family and the longing to get to know Serbia as my second home had been buried in my mind.

In the foreground, however, was the question of how to travel to Serbia together with my wife Ilse. Time and again I had to explain to my relatives why the joint venture was so difficult. They simply could not understand that we cannot leave our animals alone for a few days, or leave their care to other people. Only when I started to talk about the complicated character of our old Afghan dog "Cloé" did they seem to have some understanding. Ultimately we concluded that I should start this journey alone because of our situation.

It was a stroke of luck that Bogdan and Duzan (twins and my niece Daca's uncle) wanted to help me prepare to travel. Both had immigrated to Germany in the 1960s and found their happiness here in Reutlingen with two sisters Helga and Gitta. Bogdan and Duzan have souls of people that I have rarely met.

My suggestion to visit Serbia during the Orthodox Easter in mid-April, they found ill-advised for two reasons. First, the Serbian families have no time at all during Easter. They are totally occupied with the very extensive preparation for the holidays.

Secondly, the weather is not suitable for visitors in mid-April, because the Serbian summer is delayed. I had to agree with this argument. Ultimately, I set the travel date to mid-May, and specifically decided on the 14th to the 19th of May. Bogdan in particular gave me a lot of support during my preparation. He offered to accompany me on all trips through Serbia (with his own vehicle). In fact, he had started traveling to Belgrade one day before me.

Once again, I considered how to basically communicate my point of view to my relatives in Serbia. I did not want to create ambiguity, but that would have been the case with my English language skills and Google translate. I wanted to clarify again that I have no ambitions on any inheritances and the like. My only concern was to get to know my wonderful family better. I also clarified the problem of "gifts" with Bogdan's help. I wanted to contribute expenses for the festivities. Furthermore, it was his job to make it clear to my siblings that I would be staying overnight in a hotel.

Of course, they could not understand this request at all, because it is part of the Serbian hospitality that you spend the night in the host's house. But Bogdan stayed in the hotel as well, and consequently, everyone accepted my wishes.

Even though I had completed the rough planning for the trip by the end of December 2014, I still had to obtain my travel documents; i.e. a new passport and a new identity card had to be issued (both had expired). For reasons of cost, I booked the plane tickets at the end of 2014; the booking for the hotel "Knezevina" in Vranic near Belgrade was already under way. All appointments were perfectly coordinated with the family; the individual days and highlights were planned. I was very relieved that the problem of "gifts" for this visit was clarified.

I had worried about the children, but ultimately I purchased only a few little things for them. I planned to give my siblings Milka, Milena and Vojislav a beautiful bouquet of flowers that I had previously ordered by e-mail. Incidentally, the hotel employees must have literally read my mind about my wishes. The prices were also very moderate (for five nights with breakfast total 90 euros). The phone bill of the hotel was higher than my accommodation costs. I usually only call home to Germany. The tariffs were amazing: one minute cost over one euro!

For the record, here are the stages of a very emotional journey into my past and future.

Thursday, May 14, 2015:

09:55: Departure from Dresden Airport via Munich to Belgrade; Arrival at 14:40. After the formalities, handing over the luggage and cash exchange I moved to the exit. As always in such situations, when many people are gathered, I was struggling to recognize familiar faces. However, the "kinship delegation" (Marijana, Ace, Bogdan and Duzan had been

Ace, Duzan, me, Bogdan and Marijana

given this task.) had separated from the crowd, so I could greet everyone. They welcomed me according to the rules of Serbian hospitality. Many kisses and hugs were exchanged, and I felt very welcomed by my Serbian family.

... visiting Milena ...

Then we drove together to the apartment of my sister Milena in the center of Belgrade. She lives in a skyscraper, probably constructed in the 1950s or 60s that is in much need of renovation. The elevator was still operable and took us to the beautiful and age-appropriate apartment. For the grandchildren Andrej and Andjelko there was an extra nursery for visiting purposes. The helping hands of her daughters Daca and Maja, who looked after her, were unmistakable. Everything was very neat.

We communicated in German, otherwise English or sometimes Russian. So the hours passed and Bogdan drove me to the hotel in the evening. A beautiful but exhausting day was coming to an end, not without the hospitality of the hotel. I was so excited that I could not go to sleep yet. Instead, there were still a few cups of coffee available, which should bring the sleep!

Duzan, Bogdan, me and Ace

Friday, May 15, 2015:

The big gathering with the entire family was scheduled to start at 14:00 (2:00 pm) in Stepojevac (11 km from the hotel) at my brother Vojislav's family's home. At 11:00 Vojislav's son Dragan, wife Ljiliana and

Dragon picked up Bogdan and me from the hotel. After a short drink at the hotel and the delivery of the flowers by the hotel staff, my express wish was to once again visit my father Vitomir's grave in Stepojevac.

Whenever I stand at the grave of my father Vitomir (four times so far), I am removed from everything around me. Somehow, I am only concerned with the story of Vitomir, Frida, and myself. Such

Dragan, Dragan, Ljiliana and Bogdan

melancholy can hardly be expressed in words. At those times I feel very close to both of them. Still incomprehensible to me is that I am the result of this love story and, in addition, have revealed their best-kept secret by sheer coincidence.

We spent about two hours in the cemetery area and visited the many graves of my other relatives. But I cannot help but report a curiosity, which does not exist in Germany. Radoslav, b. 1954, is engraved on the tombstone of his wife, Danka who died in 2009, and he is already immortalized with his photo. I was so startled when I noticed his picture because I knew he was still alive! In the afternoon, he attended and seemed very

Radoslav's grave next to his wife Danka

happy to be at the family celebration. The practice of immortalizing yourself alongside your relatives during your lifetime is very common in Serbia.

In the afternoon, the entire family found themselves at Vojislav's home in Stepojevac. This time I was fortunate enough to be a little incognito because there was no newspaper, television or other acquaintances from the village and the surrounding area to greet me. So we all had a relaxing time. Since the weather was at its best, everything took place outdoors. Also all animals of the yard and the neighbors were there. The puppy dog "Njuschka" was particularly impressed with me.

Part of the Boskovic family

Siblings

Trojka Mark, Milica, John

As Ilse would soon be celebrating her 70th birthday at home in Germany, we had come up with something special. Marijana had baked a giant cake (about 80 x 60 cm) with the inscription "For Ilse's 70th birthday". This cake figuratively brought Ilse to Stepojevac, where we enjoyed eating

Round Table

together. After we ate, we made a greeting video for Ilse in which all attendees had their say (in German, English and Serbian). In the middle was this beautiful masterpiece by Marijana.

Vojislav, Milica and me

Radoslav (the son of my deceased sister Milunka, who died 2002) asked me to visit his house and his family, which is also in Stepojevac. I knew that with the best of intentions, I could not refuse his invitation, so we promised to "stop by." My time grew short, and a lot of other visits were waiting for me.

At around 8 o'clock, we said goodbye to each other in Serbian style and off we went back to the hotel, no trace of rest. During a long walk around the hotel, I again reviewed the events of the day. I was too excited to get "horizontal." At about

11:00 pm I ended the day with a strong coffee, including some goodies that the friendly waiter still served. The next day was full of encounters again.

Saturday, May 16, 2015:

We traveled to Sevojno, about 150 km away (near Uzice), a small village in the low mountain range where my dear family Jovanovic lived and ran a strawberry, raspberry and vegetable stand. Ace (with his car), Dragan, and Bogdan escorted me there. We left the hotel at 10am because we were expected to arrive at 2pm.

Vitomir (my father), Frida (my mother) and grandmother Spasenja, the eternally living

Part of the Jovanovic family

As a precaution, I limited our visit to a maximum of three hours, which did not particularly appeal to the Jovanovics. Unfortunately, to fulfill all my visiting appointments, I had no choice. On the way back to the hotel, we had to make a trip to Radoslav. In short, it was another wonderful afternoon in the company of my friends, the Jovanovic family (Sascha, Ankica, mother Kose, the children Sandra and Miroslav and Natasha, a relative). I must rave about the dishes and drinks. The highlight was again a giant cake with a lot of cream, fresh strawberries and other goodies. The guests were joined by a father and son of the neighbor, who had lived in Germany for a long time and who also had much to say. However, the Serbian difficulties that have to be overcome have been discussed again and again. Although enthusiastic about Germany, most of them want to stay in their Serbian homeland.

On my insistence, we drove punctually an hour later again in the direction of Stepojevac/Belgrade. We reached the Radoslav's house in the early evening, quite exhausted.

We stayed for about an hour, enjoyed their hospitality (again with delicious food and drinks) with another invitation for the next morning as we said goodbye. This was possible because we were not expected until afternoon in Belgrade with Miljkovic's family.

German-Connection in Sevojno

Everything in my head went haywire. How can we do justice to each family's invitation and not neglect anyone?
If we were on time, we could visit each for a few hours. Is there such a thing in Serbia?
In the late evening we drove back to the hotel, with a really short detour at Vojislav's house in Stepojevac. This time I had only one thing in mind: getting "horizontal."

Sunday, May 17, 2015:

At 3 pm the Miljkovics invited us to Belgrade. After the DNA tests proved that her father Radojica (Zeppelin) was unfortunately not my father, we had a lot of friendly contact with the family of Natalija and Branislava. They had made me promise to visit them every time I visit Serbia. Since we have many things in common, they would have liked to have been my siblings.

For the Radoslav's family visit, I only had a time window of a maximum of 3 hours, ie from 10 am to 1 pm. That's why we started early. At 9 o'clock Dragan appeared in the lobby with Ljiljana, Milica and Mark to accompany me.

We stopped to drink coffee (but I had already had breakfast), so we immediately went to the Ravoslav's family (there were Ravoslav's son Milos and daughter-in-law Marija, their twins Nina and Lena and the other Daughter Marija, accompanied by Radoslav's sister Ranka with son Ivan, daughter-in-law Mladena and two children

Andrea and Alex). Incidentally, I would not be able to enumerate all the many names and family relationships if I did not constantly carry my "family tree" with me, which I had to complete. Since time was very short, it was almost time for the "feasting" or whatever you call it. When a guest comes to

Parts of Radoslav's family and some guests

visit, something special is always on the table. I hardly believe that in everyday life, the Serbian family exerts so much effort for meals.

"

Beginning of a "calorie-free food intake

Can one say no?

Nevertheless, during these few hours I was able to talk intensively to Radoslav and his family. He was able to contribute much information from my father Vitomir's unknown cache. For example, I received as a gift a POW coupon for free shopping in the prisoner of war camp (see page 14).

Time flew by, and Dragan took me to the hotel, where I only had a short time to change my clothes because I was drenched in sweat from the temperature outdoors. I also wanted to make a good impression on Professor Branislava and Natalija (high school teacher) in Belgrade.

On time, at 3 pm, Bogdan delivered me to the Miljkovics.. He was also welcome as a guest.

We were greeted very eagerly. Immediately, we exchanged intense conversation about the wellbeing of all and swapped events about the everyday life of our respective families. Also, we reviewed some episodes of my search because I had finally found my father's family. In addition, I had to make a promise to bring my wife Ilse on my next visit. As always on such occasions, the living room table played a dominant role. It was served up with what the kitchen, cellar and market had made. Of course everything was calorie-free, as the photo proves. But delicious, delicious, delicious! Even after of several hours past supper, it is still the highpoint of all epicurean events.

Because the three of us would have liked to become siblings, we had to justify the negative DNA results. Nevertheless, somehow we are connected by an invisible bond of friendship, which is underpinned by my thesis that "Zeppelin" was intensely friendly with my mother.

"Siblings in friendship"
(left:Branislava, right:Natalija)

As always, the few hours went by quickly. Bogdan again took over the drive back to the hotel. By the way, my wish to travel sometimes by bus was strictly rejected. Here I would like to thank Marijana, Ace, Dragan and Bogdan and all others for their helpfulness. During these days, they drove me several hundred kilometers and for hours through the surrounding area of Belgrade to visit my acquaintances, friends and relatives.

Monday, May 18, 2015:

The fifth day of my trip was fully planned. The afternoon was reserved for a visit to Marijana and Ace in Belgrade. In the morning I wanted to meet with good friends; Velinka, Radmila and Diniku. We chose the hotel's restaurant as the meeting place after the Diniku's suggestion of meeting in Zrenjanin (where Velinka lives)70 km away, was rejected as a possibility. Bogdan immediately pointed out that all of our appointments for the day would have become unmanageable, because Velinka's family would certainly have arranged a big party for me that would require our being there for a long time. I've known Velinka for over a year, but only through emails, Skype and phone. She had asked me to look for her brother Peter. Her father,

Radmila and Velnka (from left)

Radovan Blazic, was a prisoner of war in Oderwitz. In the next chapter I will go into more detail. After they learned about my visit to Serbia, they naturally wanted to get to know me personally.

At that point, everyone was still hopeful that Veginka would soon find her brother. Unfortunately, the DNA test was negative and the search had to continue. Marijana was invited for dinner that afternoon. Ace picked me up from the hotel. Since we had about an hour left, he took me to the beautiful recreational park in Belgrade, a beautiful landscape with many trees, various restaurants and especially a huge lake with a beautiful sandy beach in the middle of a big city.

We took a seat outside a restaurant in huge armchairs and enjoyed our coffee under Mediterranean plants. After Marijana had given the cell phone "green light" for the finished meal, we went immediately to their large luxurious villa. Bogdan and Dragan were also present. The sons Filip and Igor, his wife Jelena and the 10-month-old "Sweety" Nina joined the group.

Ace and Marijana on the balcony of their villa

Again we enjoyed the proverbial hospitality of my Serbian relatives. Bogdan and Dragan skillfully overruled my linguistic difficulties. In short: this afternoon will remain with me as a beautiful memory. Igor's small family with his wonderful wife Jelena and the little whirlwind Nina gave these hours a living frame.

Since Ace was prevented, Marijana drove me back to the hotel. Another short "nightcap" in the form of a pot of coffee and off we went to the well-deserved night's sleep.

The last day, like all the past days of my visit, should start with surprises.

Igor, Jelena und Nina

and again just a little "hospitality"

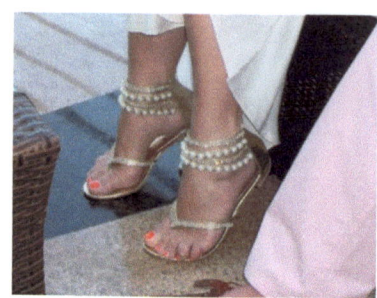

...she will check to verify that I included this photo ...

from another star,- Marijana

Tuesday, May 19, 2015:

This time, however, I experienced a nasty surprise. Because I knew I was going to say goodbye and I had not packed my suitcase, I got up quite early. Somehow, my head felt foggy and a strong, intensely-sweet smell was spreading around the room. I checked on and under the desk, the television stand, and handled various items such as my dictionaries, laundry bags, glasses and the like. I touched a mass that felt like thin syrup. The bottle of home-baked Raki, which Radoslav had given me as a farewell present, had exploded probably because the alcoholic beverage had fermented beyond the bottle's capacity.

Fortunately, the actual damage was limited. After I cleared away most of the foul-smelling drink on myself with water and toilet paper, a housekeeper helped me restore order. Hopefully, she was happy with the 10-euro bill I left on my freshly made bed. While she worked, I could have breakfast. When I returned to the room, I sacrificed at least half a bottle of the best aftershave, so that, with good conscience, I was able to hand over my beautiful room in a reasonably decent condition.

The last day had begun. In summary, I must reiterate that I once again was allowed to enjoy the unlimited warmth and hospitality of my family and friends. At least seven times, "eat it up, it won't keep" was repeated. Oddly, I did not gain a single gram. Before my flight, I settled my hotel bill in the lobby: telephone costs and flowers (9 bouquets a 10 €). With great melancholy, I thought of having to say goodbye.

We had a few hours left before my departure. Marijana had promised me a goodbye surprise. There were several surprises, but this time they were all positive. A large contingent of my family appeared in the hotel. Traveling in four vehicles, ten members of the Boskovic family hugged me once again, in formal Serbian fashion ("tyssjaci poljubaci"). It was a heartbreaking scenario, with many tears and good wishes. My sisters Milka and Milena, the "Germans" Bogdan and Dragan, the nephews Bogdan and wife Ljiljana and Radoslav with girlfriend Milena and niece Marijana with her sister Gordana made every effort to increase the difficulty of my departure.

Marijana handed me her second surprise. She had literally "fought" the Central Archive in Belgrade (see page 93) to obtain significant documents for my father's family tree. The travel window for me to get to the airport was blown. Alone, Marijana would drive me to the airport. What an honor for me !!! After the luggage was stowed, we could start. As we drove away, I stole a quick look back at the waving crowd and these beautiful days were gone. Marijana drove me to the entrance of the airport; where she was forbidden to stop! Such rules did not matter to her; greetings to Ilse, kiss three times and she was gone. I stood there, rooted to the spot, trying to grasp again the implications of this visit. What wonderful people I had the opportunity to experience a second time.
2:40pm flight via Zurich with arrival at 7:50 in Dresden.

Back in my homeland and with my family, I had to allow the many experiences and incidents sink in. After a few days, I realized I had to write another book. Ilse had previously suggested that I needed to write about the search for my father Vitomir. In my first book, I had already laid foundation for this search in the seventh chapter. However, it was both of our convictions that my story was probably unique, considering the circumstances of my birth and how I discovered the information. We did not want to withhold this knowledge not only from our descendants, but also from the public.

In the meantime, we received the message that my brother Vojislav had a serious fall and was in the hospital. He had surgery on his thigh (his hip was not fractured). After a few days he was able to leave the hospital, probably because of financial concerns, and was cared for in his Stepojevac home. Because of his impaired mobility, his being home was not an easy task. In order to help him, Dragan took a few days off from work. In the meantime, his relatives had found a nursing home in Obrenovac (not far from Belgrade and Stepojevac). It was certainly the best solution. On the internet, I was able to research that the local gerontology center has a very good reputation and the senior citizens are well cared for there. For his birthday, I sent him a small gift, a photo album. According to his daughter Duzanka, he was very happy with the album. Subsequently, all the doctors, nurses and caregivers were then told about our wonderful story. Surely, that appreciation gave his recovery a great boost. On the actual day of his birthday, we were able to make a telephone connection with the nursing home, and the telephone was taken to Vojislav's bedside. Ilse and I trilled the melody "Happy birthday to you ..." and spoke a few sentences in Serbian. He was speechless, only was able to respond with a hearty "Hvala" (Thanks).

Genealogy Family Boskovic:

Anyone who has ever constructed a family tree knows that one's genealogy is never complete. Additional people are always discovered and added; mainly because of the excellent Internet program "My Heritage."

After my first visit to Serbia, I started to research my family history starting with my father Vitomir (Born: 1907, Died: 1993). Again, it is easier said than done. A year ago, I could not imagine how to proceed. It soon became clear to me that there are bureaucratic hurdles in that area of Serbia.

Here are some of my activities:

At the end of 2013, I stepped up my search for my Serbian ancestors. On the Internet I found a lot of evidence that Vitomir's ancestral record goes back a long way, through South East Europe to 11th century Austria and continues to the 16th century. In the south of Czechoslovakia, there is the small town of Boskovice with about 11,000 inhabitants. In all probability, it was founded around 1030 by a member of my family. After discovering these facts, my research urge increased.

Using a pre-translated text, I sought information from various offices, churches and public institutions in Stepojevac, Lazarevac and Belgrade. I finally succeeded in connecting with Snezena Zivanovic from Lazarevac's municipal office. She confirmed that she would be personally present at my next visit.

I also asked the hotel staff in Vranic for help. They talked to the priest of Stepojevac about Vitomir. Unfortunately, I received no response from the church. Repeatedly, Daca and Ljiljana tried to help me with no success. I had the feeling that no one from the state or the church was willing to give me any information. Now I know why my suspicions were correct.

The reasons go back more than 70 years. But before I discovered those reasons, I used my "secret weapon" or my "Sherlock Holmes," my dear family Jovanovic from Sevojno, who assisted me in the search for my father. They sent me a whole series of telephone connections, addresses and e-mail addresses of churches and institutions. A Mrs. Slavica Petkovic from the Church Office in Belgrade also provided contact information. From the information gleaned from these sources, I determined the following:

For all those born after 1911, a central registry was introduced in Serbia.
For those born before 1911, there were three possibilities:
    a) Some of the documents were in Lazarevac.
    b) Another part is handled in Stepojevac's registry office.
    c) Everything that happened before 1879 is kept in the Historical Archives in
    Belgrade.

With that information, I could find out which variant applied to my questions.
Lazarevac, Stepojevac and the churches had given me no information. After
receiving no reponse from the State Archives in Belgrade, my niece Marijana came
into play as the next "Weapon of Weapons." With her stunning charm, she melts all
blocks of ice and overcomes impregnable fortresses in an instant.

Researching the Historical Archives of Belgrade, she actually managed to trace back
the Boskovic line until circa 1785. She even obtained certified copies of documents,
despite the fact that the official demanded a general power of attorney from me.
Without further ado, Marijana herself signed a certificate in which she confirmed
that she was using these documents for personal purposes only. At that point, it
became clear to me, that the Serbian institutions were not allowed to issue
documents to foreigners, let alone to Germans. The offices fear litigation over such
things as inheritances, etc. Such concerns are irrelevant in my case, however,
because I have always stated that I make no demands on my father and his family.

A brief overview shows the chronology of Boskovics:
    1. **My father Vitomir** (Born: September 26, 1907, Died April 30, 1993)
    2. **Grandfather Sreten** (Born: October 04, 1885, Died 1918, dropped?)
    3. **Great-grandfather Mihailo** (Born: October 29, 1861, Died: ?)
    4. **Great-grandfather Pavle** (Born: 1830, Died: March 23, 1896)
    5. **Great-great-grandfather Valisilje** (Born: 1785, Died: March 21, 1854)

Marijana gave me a veritable treasure trove of documents and memorabilia, e.g.
excerpts from church books. From the Jovanovics, I received birth and death
certificates for Vitomir and Sreten. From my Stepojevac family, I received the
original photos of me and Frida, the military passport of Vitomir and a receipt book
detailing paid rent/property tax to the community from 1929 to 1931.

My dear Bogdan from Reutlingen also had some memories of Vitomir. During our
acquaintance, he still remembered many details. With the end of this chapter, I
would like to emphasize a particular statement: **"Frida cared for Vitomir when
he injured his back, and was dying of illness!"**

Chapter 5 - You do not live alone in this world
Or: How do I help other people to their happiness.

When I became a quasi-public person after my story appeared on television, newspaper, and book, many people from Serbia, Austria, Switzerland, Croatia and Germany, appealed to me to help them find their fathers, siblings and relatives. I physically empathized with their inner need, their hopes regarding who their people were/are and to search for their origin. Here are just a few of my "achievements":

- Hildegard Wagner from Sebnitz found the family of her Serbian father Simu Pustinja (Brother Branko and Sister Milica). She visited her family in Serbia, and on her 70th birthday, a family delegation from Zrenjanin came to her celebration. Ilse and I were present as invited guests. To look into the happy faces of all these happy people has made up, many times over, for the many researching troubles.

- Mrs. Vladislava Bogdanovic from Bosnia asked to find her brother Josef in Austria. Her father Josip Bogdanovic was imprisoned there and left a child. No one had contacted anyone until my story became known in Bosnia. After just one day, I was able to establish the connection between the siblings. Again, the reactions were very positive and they were getting to know each other.

- Many inquiries are still in progress, such as with Mrs. Christine Waschwill from Chemnitz, who is looking for her Ukrainian father Ivan Lutsenko (born: 1925). Surely these stories will also be the subject of a new book, as the most wondrous events accompany that search (for example, contact with the Thai princes and the royal family).

Chapter 6 - Epilogue

In the last four years, my life has changed fundamentally. A big new Serbian family has entered my everyday life. Only in the past few months has my daily routine become somewhat normal. My day no longer starts by retrieving e-mails from Serbia, but now, as many obstacles have been removed and the Stepojevac and Belgrade families have become an integral part of my family, I am devoting myself to other areas of focus. In my heart, however, I still find that a part of myself wanders into my past. I imagine how it must have been when Frida and Vitomir loved each other in such a terrible time. Then I see the photos of the farmhouse and the barn where everything must have happened. Then I also think back to how my search for my father began and where I had achieved partial successes, and then landed in some dead end. It's still a big mystery to me that randomly, rational and generous people are still helping me in the search. Hopefully, the present book will also be a stimulus and incentive for people with a similar fate and have not yet managed to go through the long and difficult path of knowledge. However, one should always remember that every human being has the right to know his roots. On the path of knowledge, you often have to accept setbacks, but success brings a new life to you.

Finally, I would like to thank my wife, Ilse, for giving me the strength and support to not give up my search.

References

, P.125 / 126 - Photos were taken during the broadcast of the MDR on 28.11.2014

, P.22 - graphic "whales" from the Internet of "Wikipedia"

, P.33 - Newspaper article from the "Stollberger Zeitung" from 17.11.2011

, P.44 - Excerpts from the Serbian newspaper "blic"

, S 45 - Article from the "Stollberger Freie Presse"

, Pp. 70, 79, 80 - Results of DNA tests from a Belgrade institute

, All other photos came from personal sources